Ocean and Sea Coloring Book

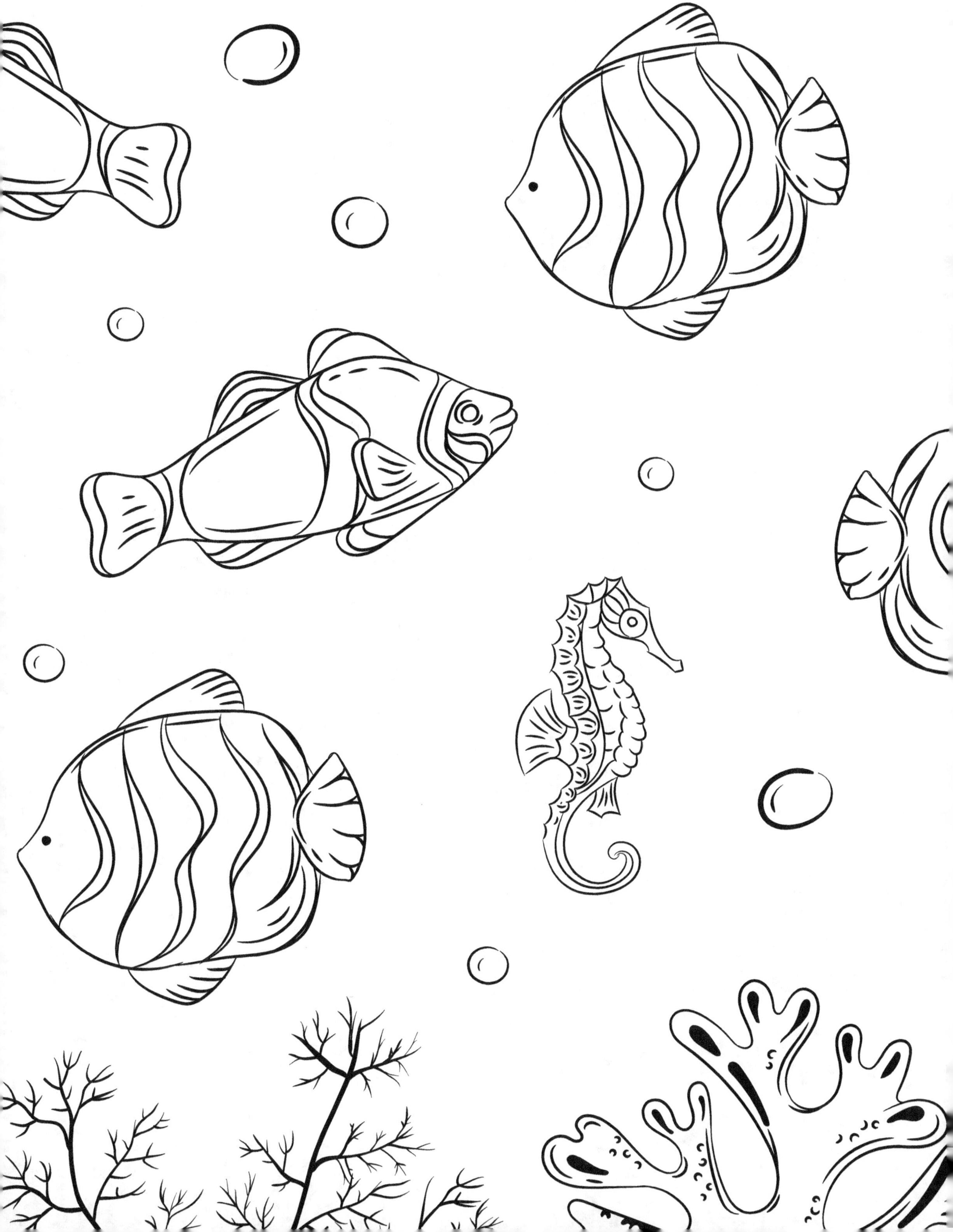

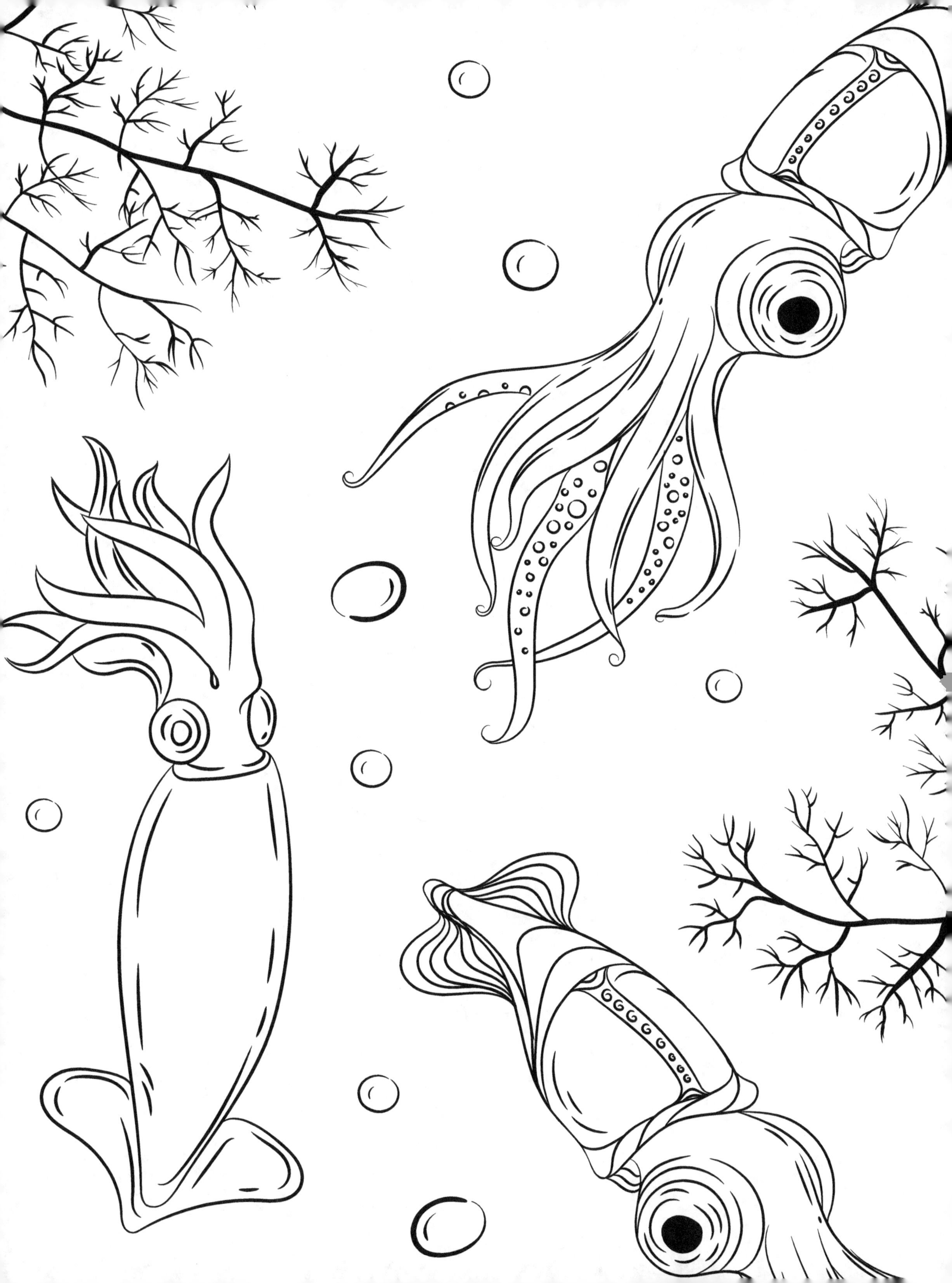

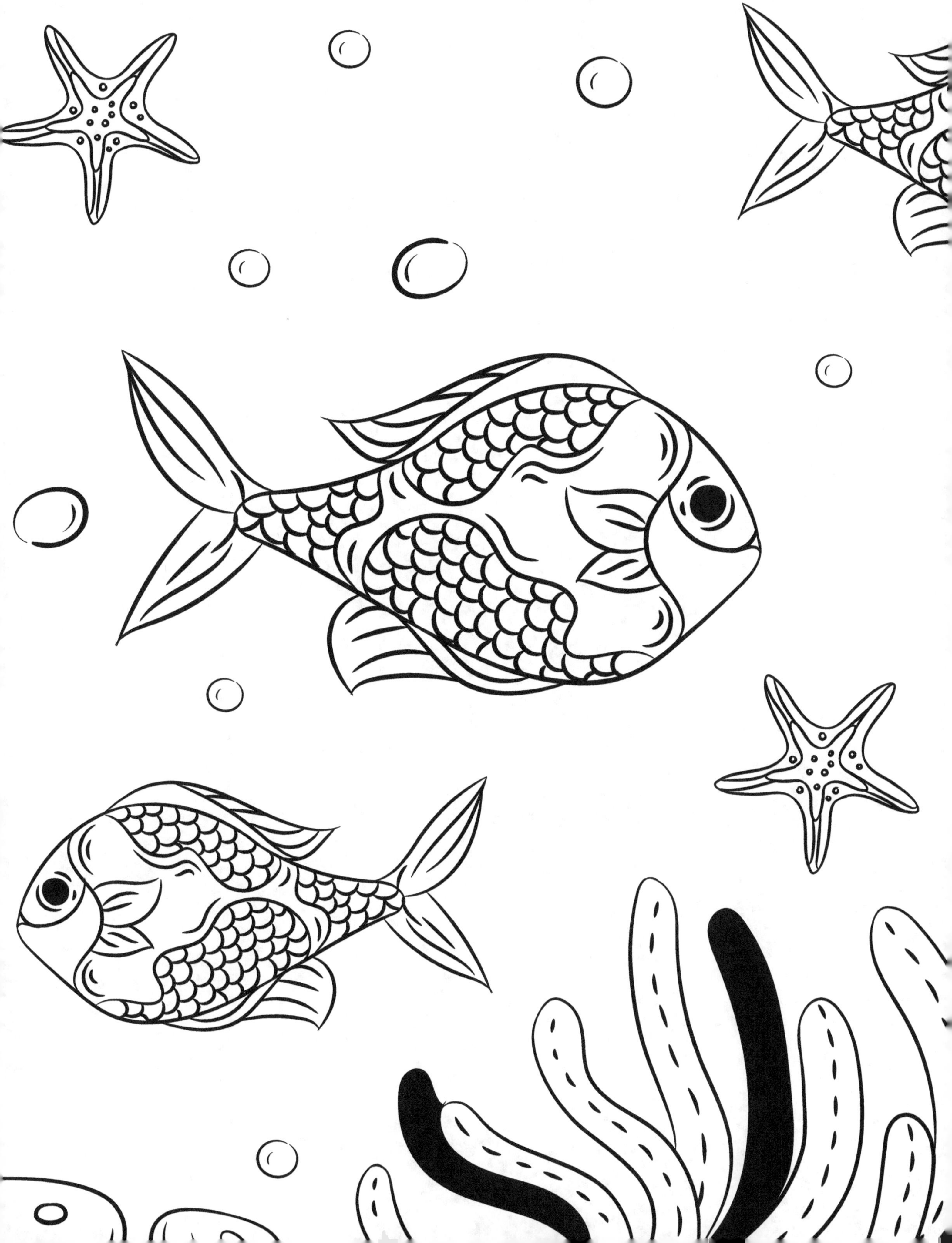

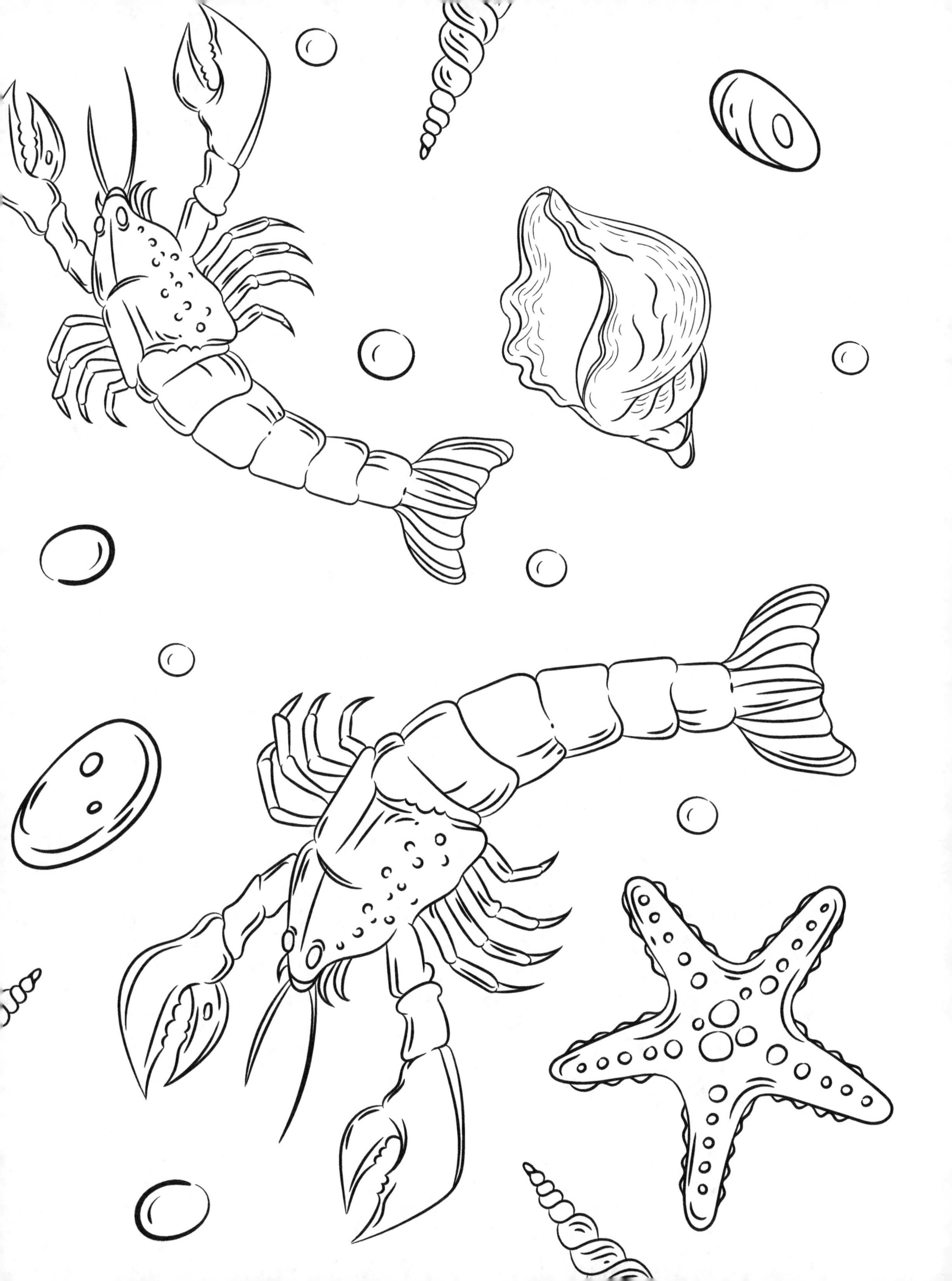

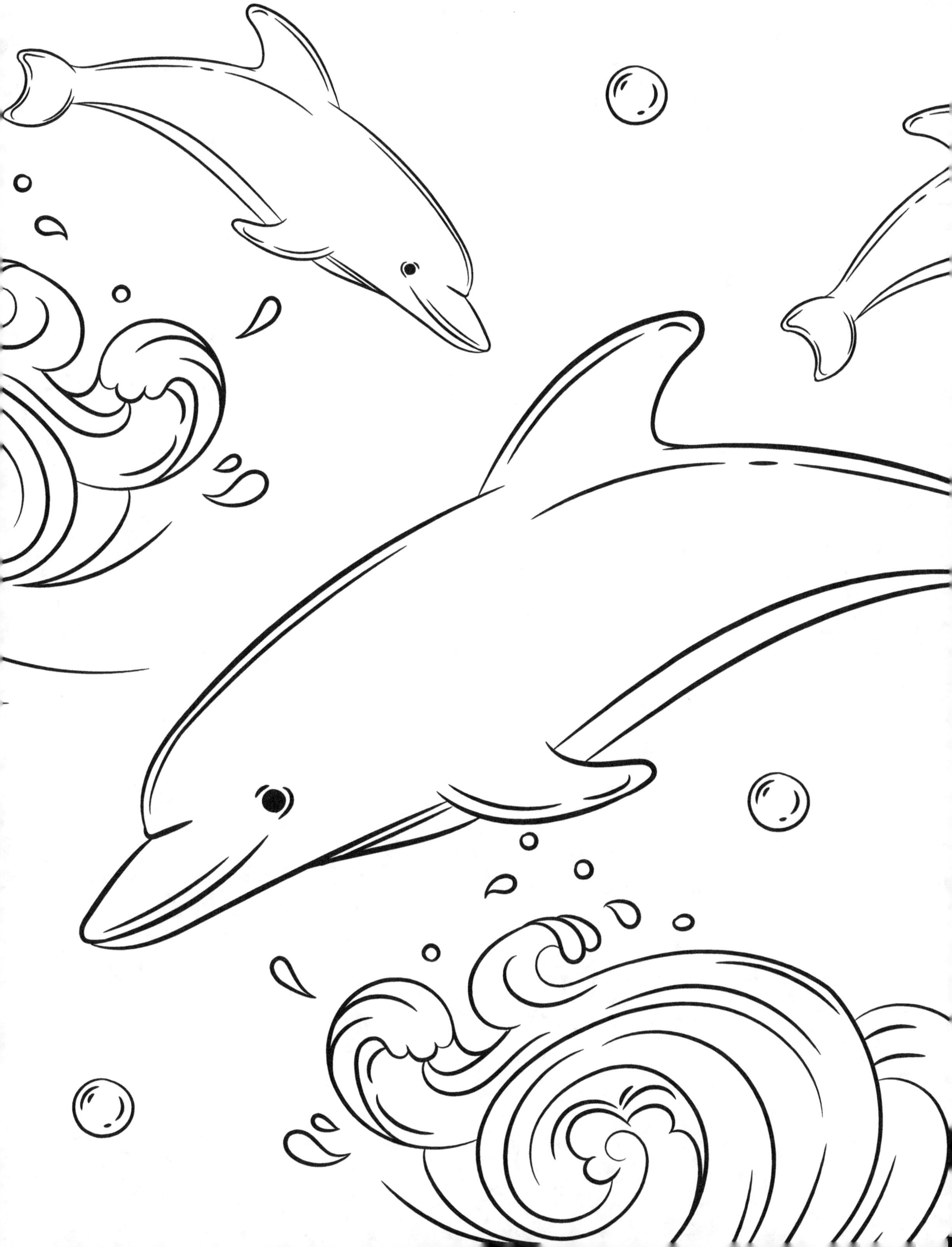

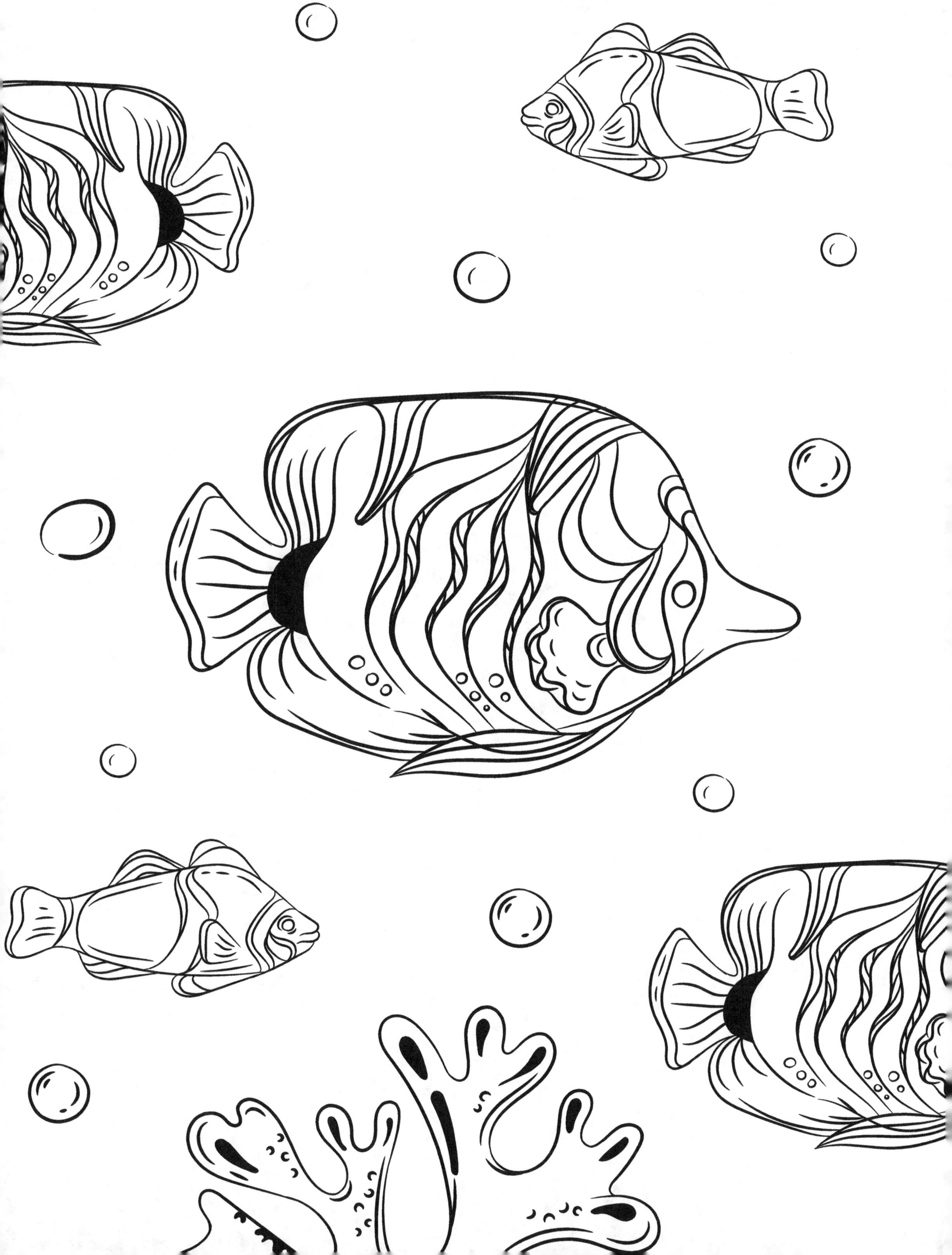

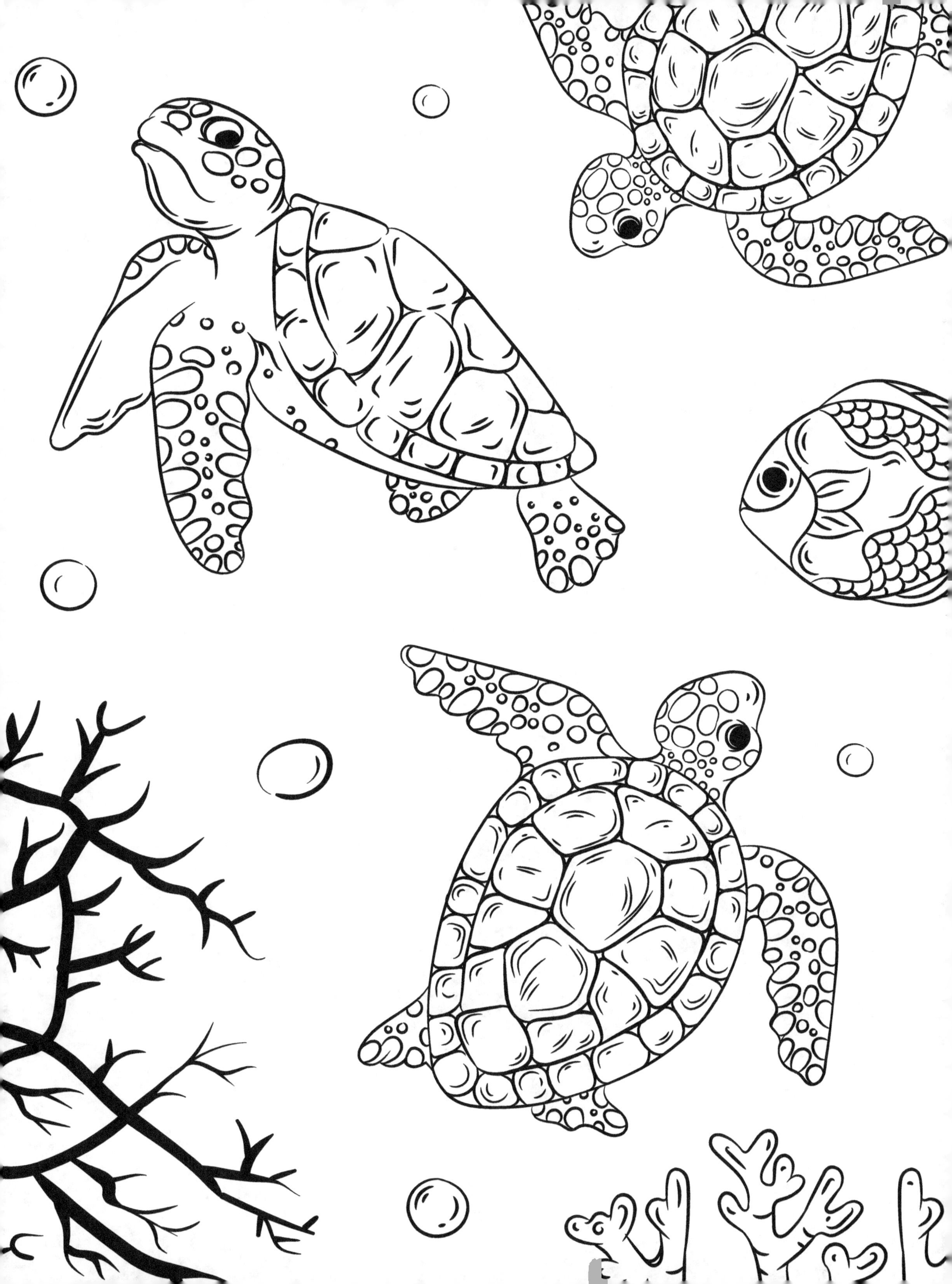

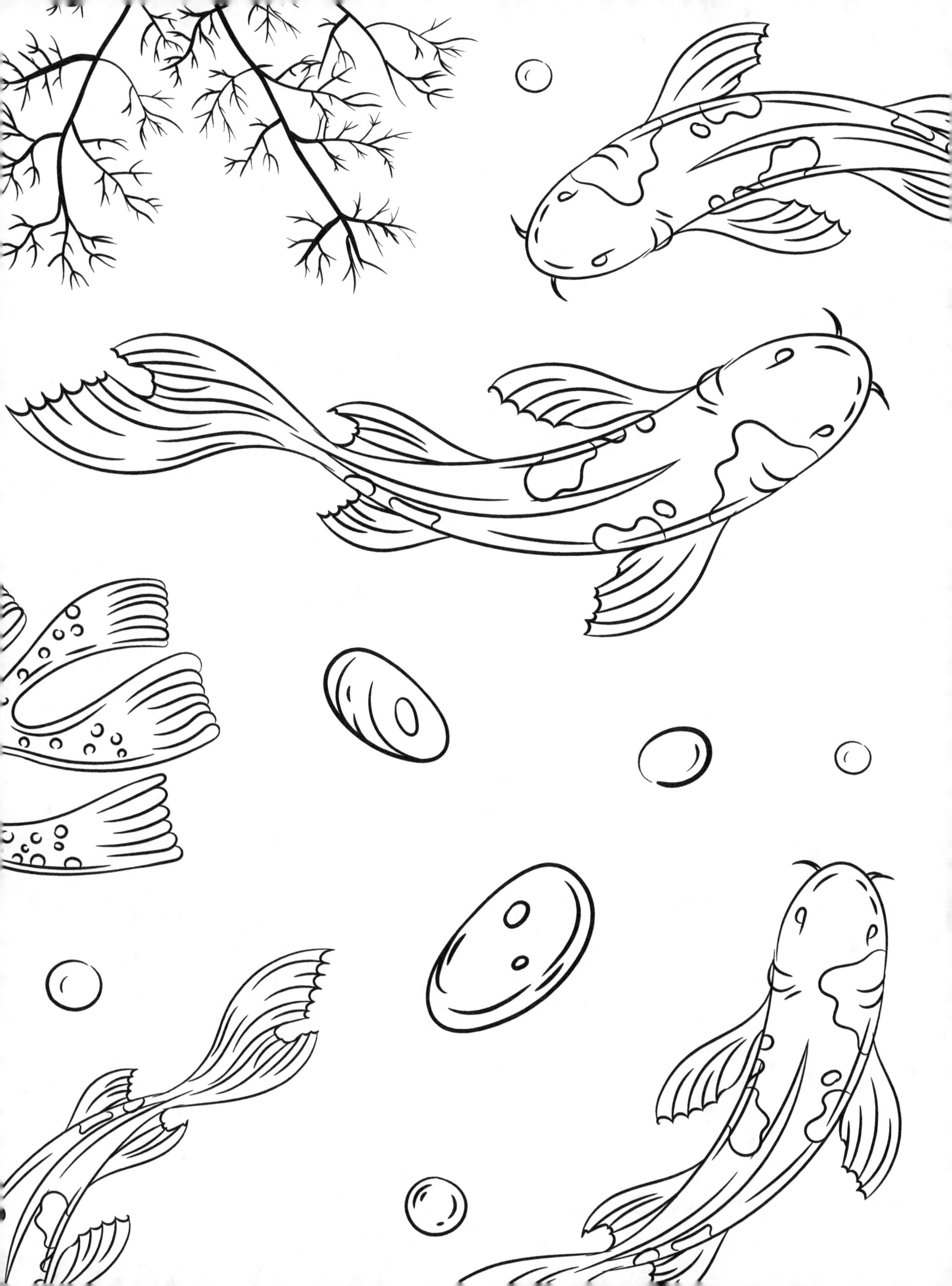

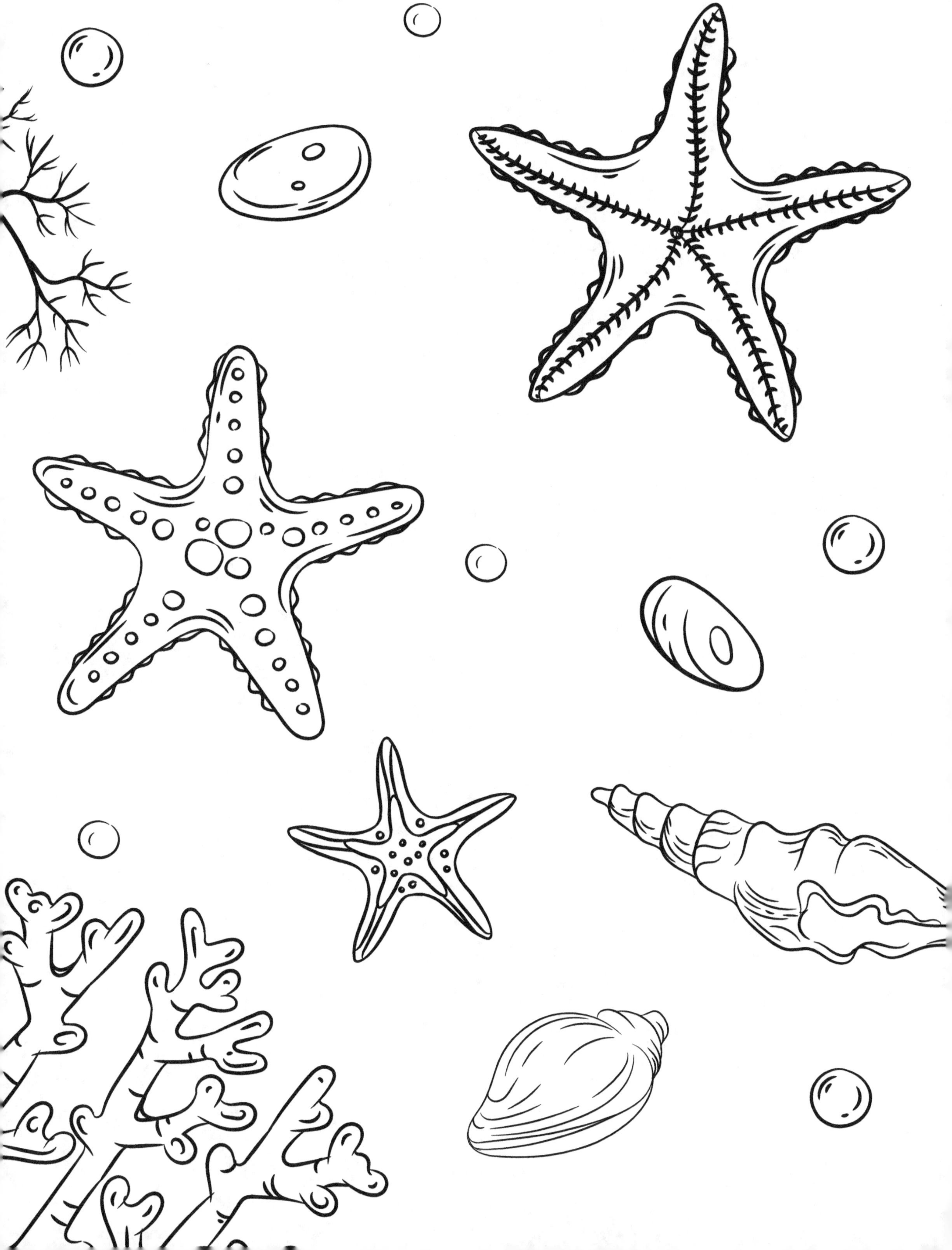

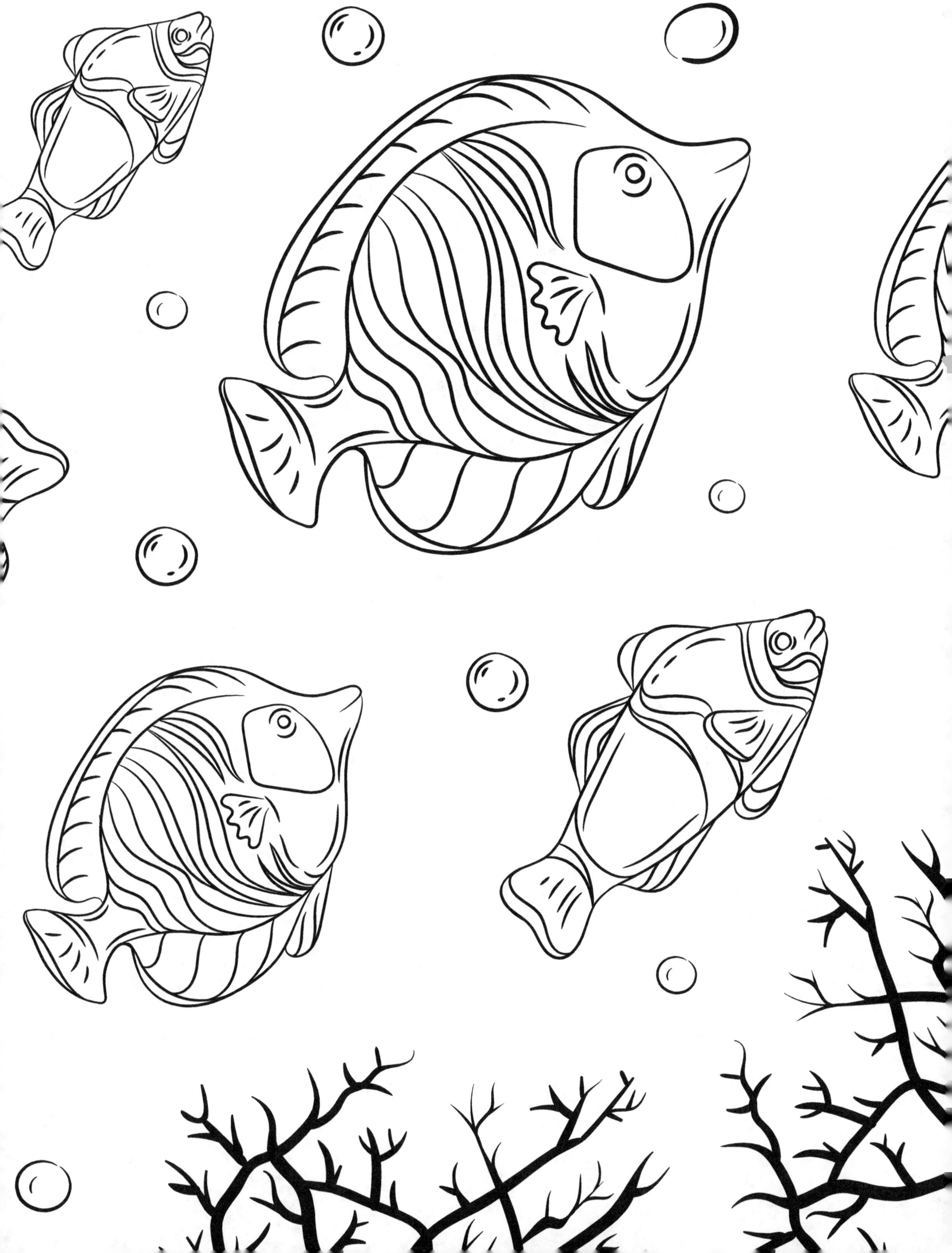

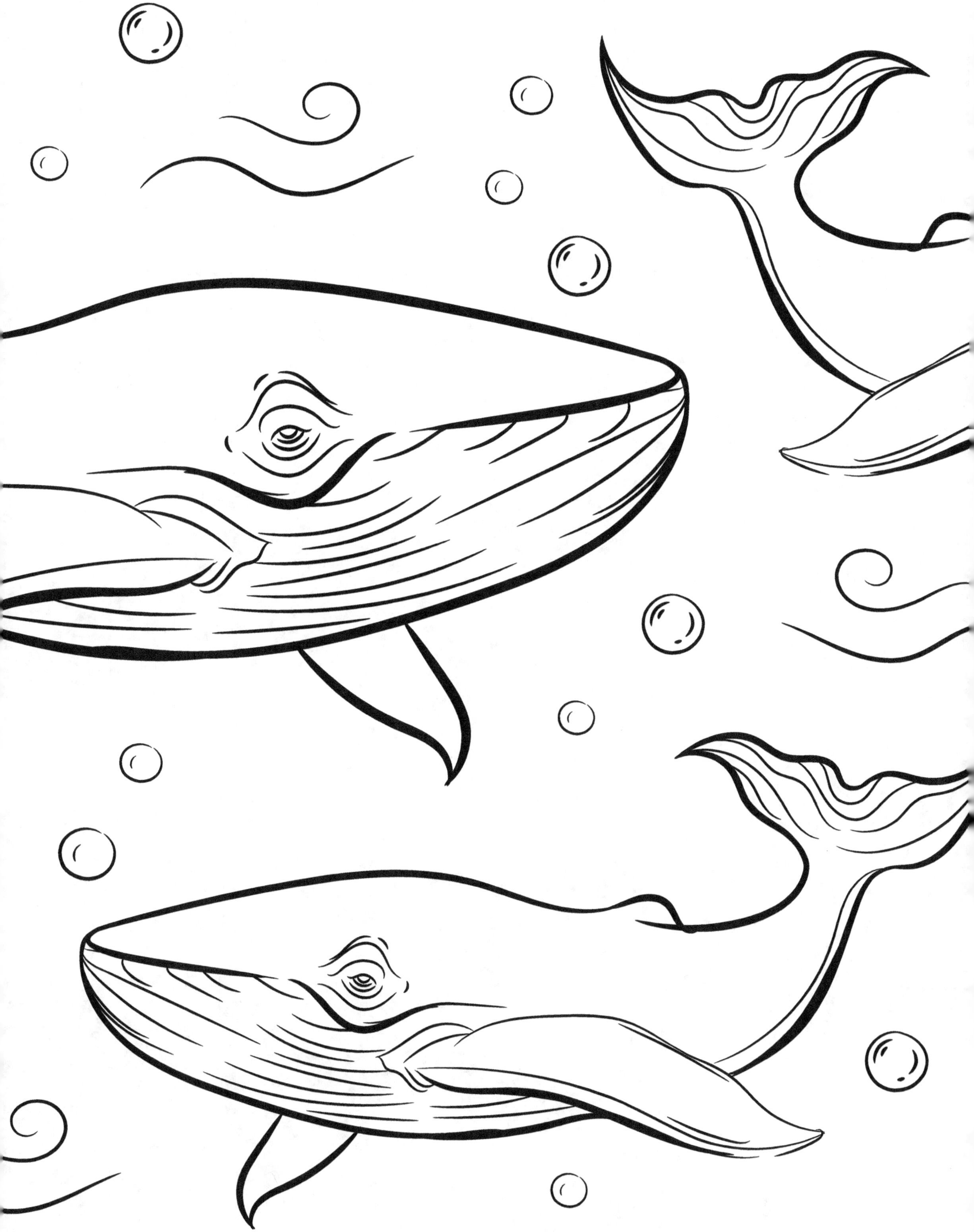

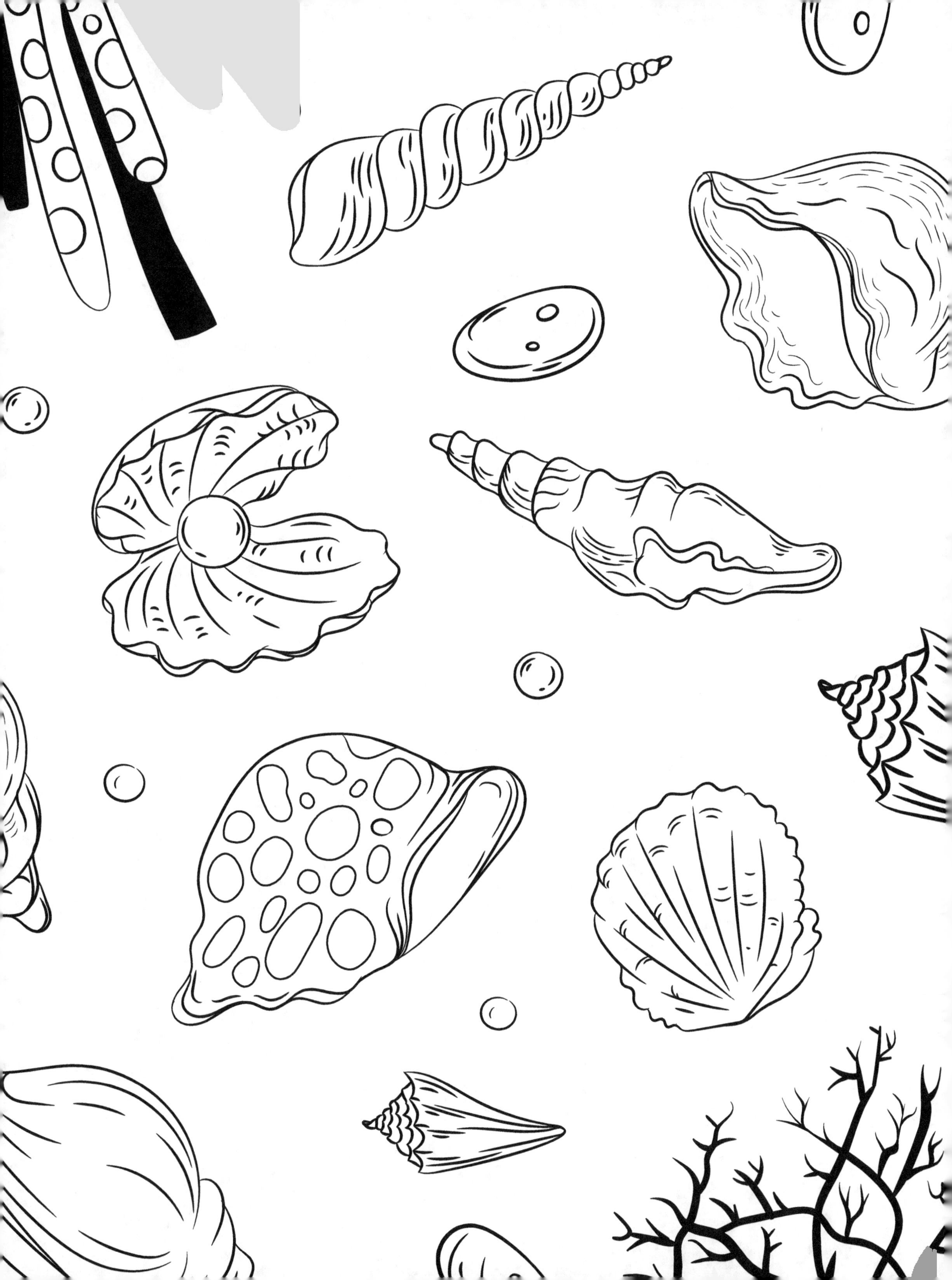

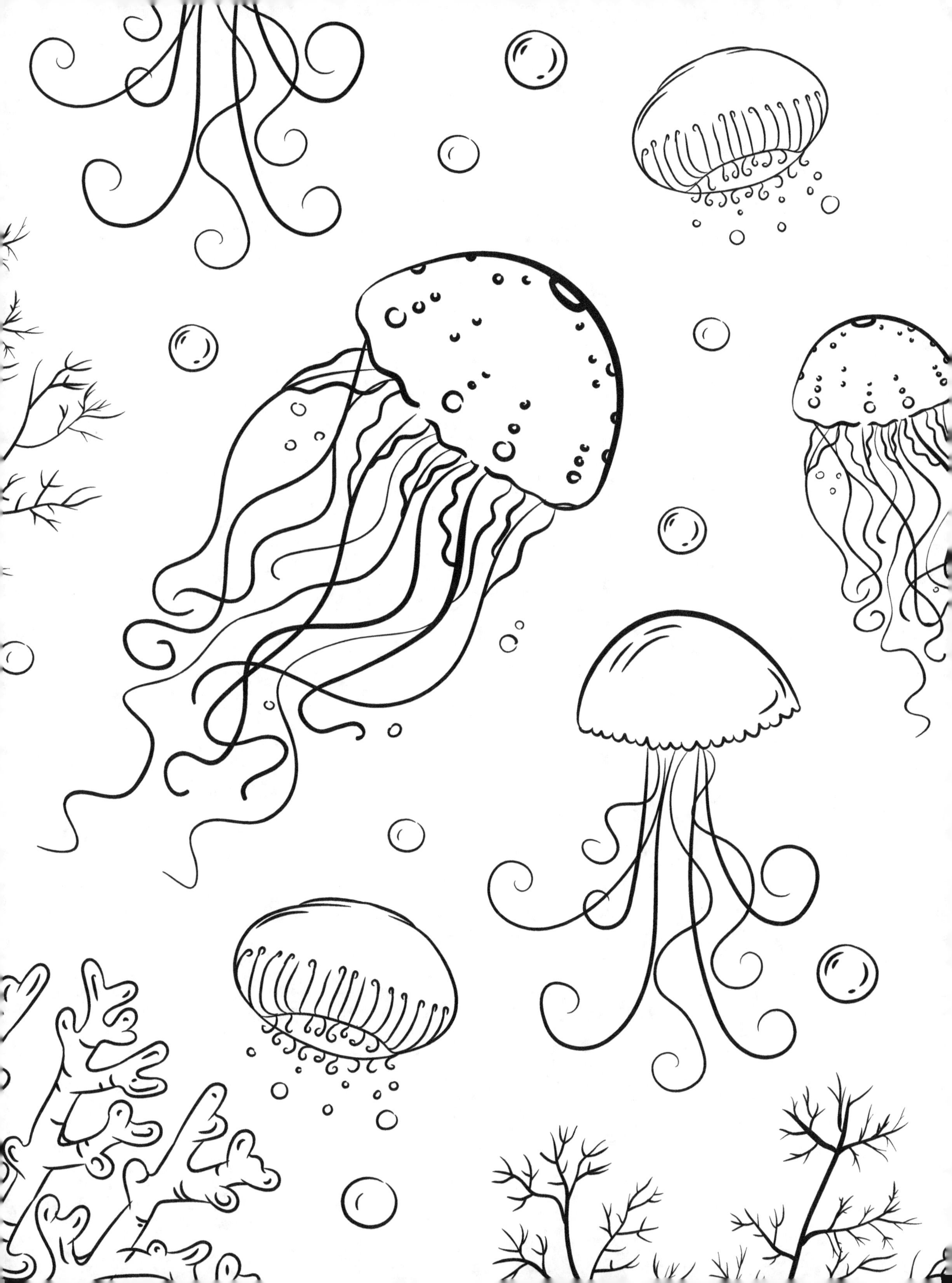

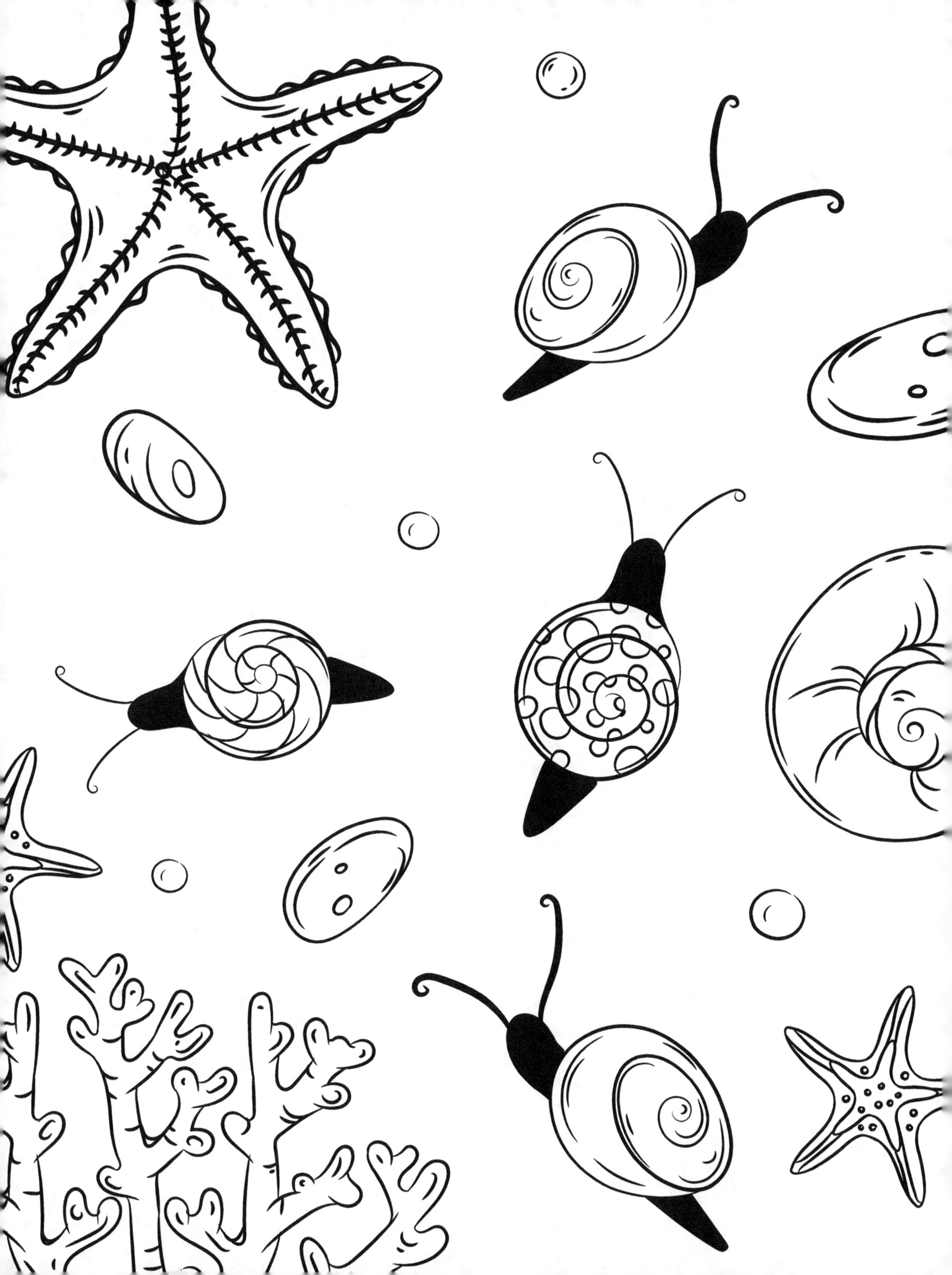

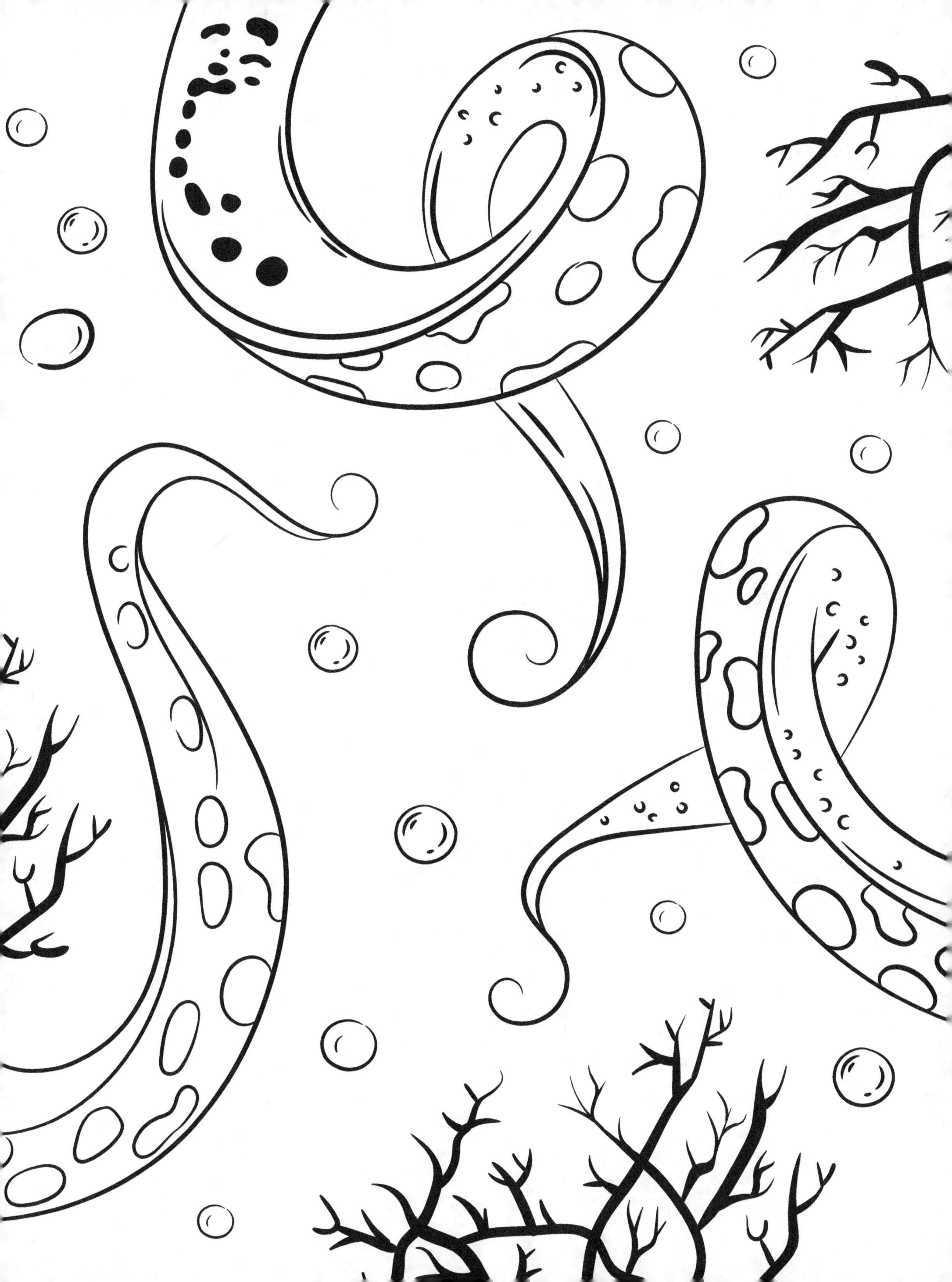

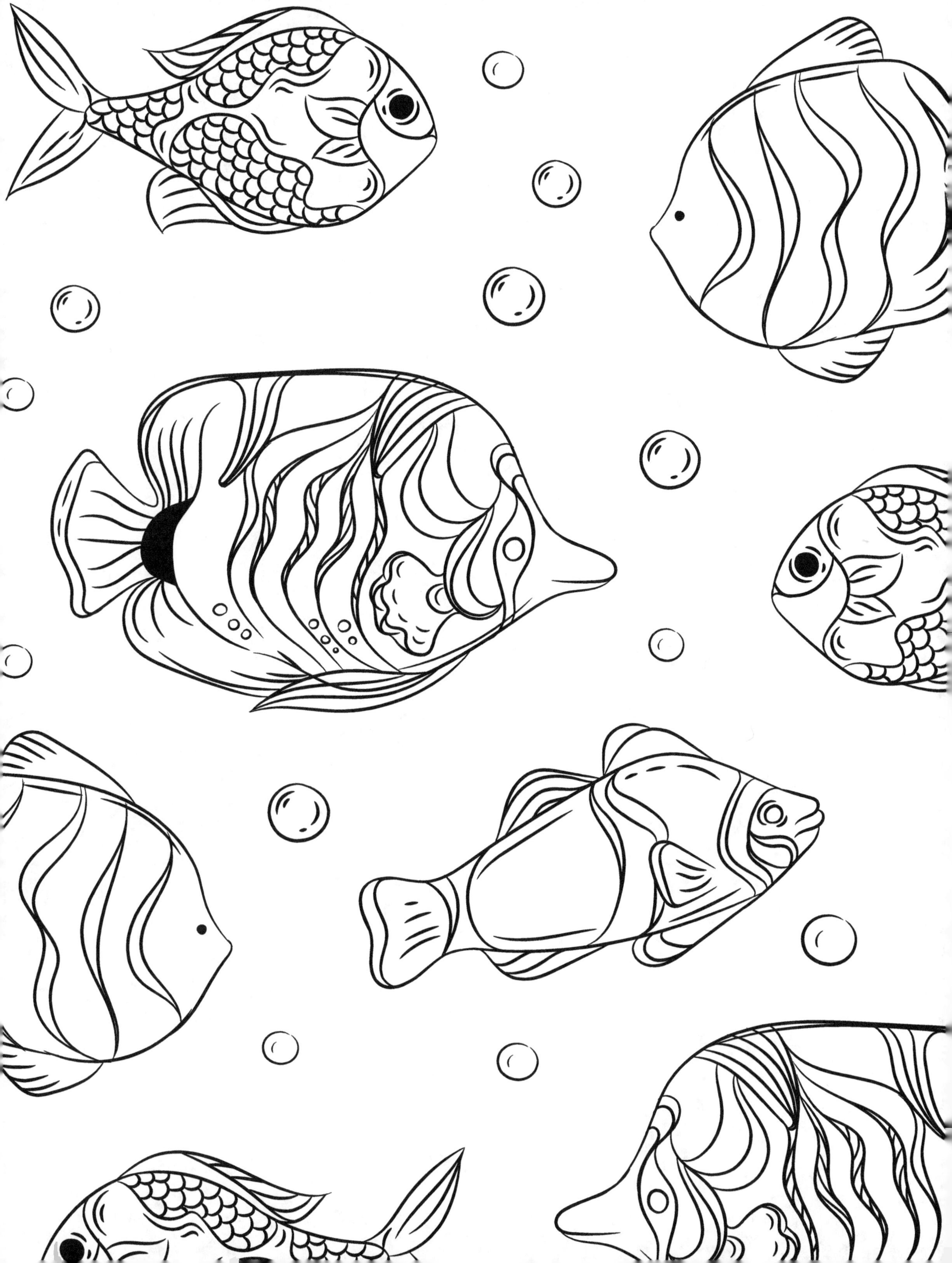

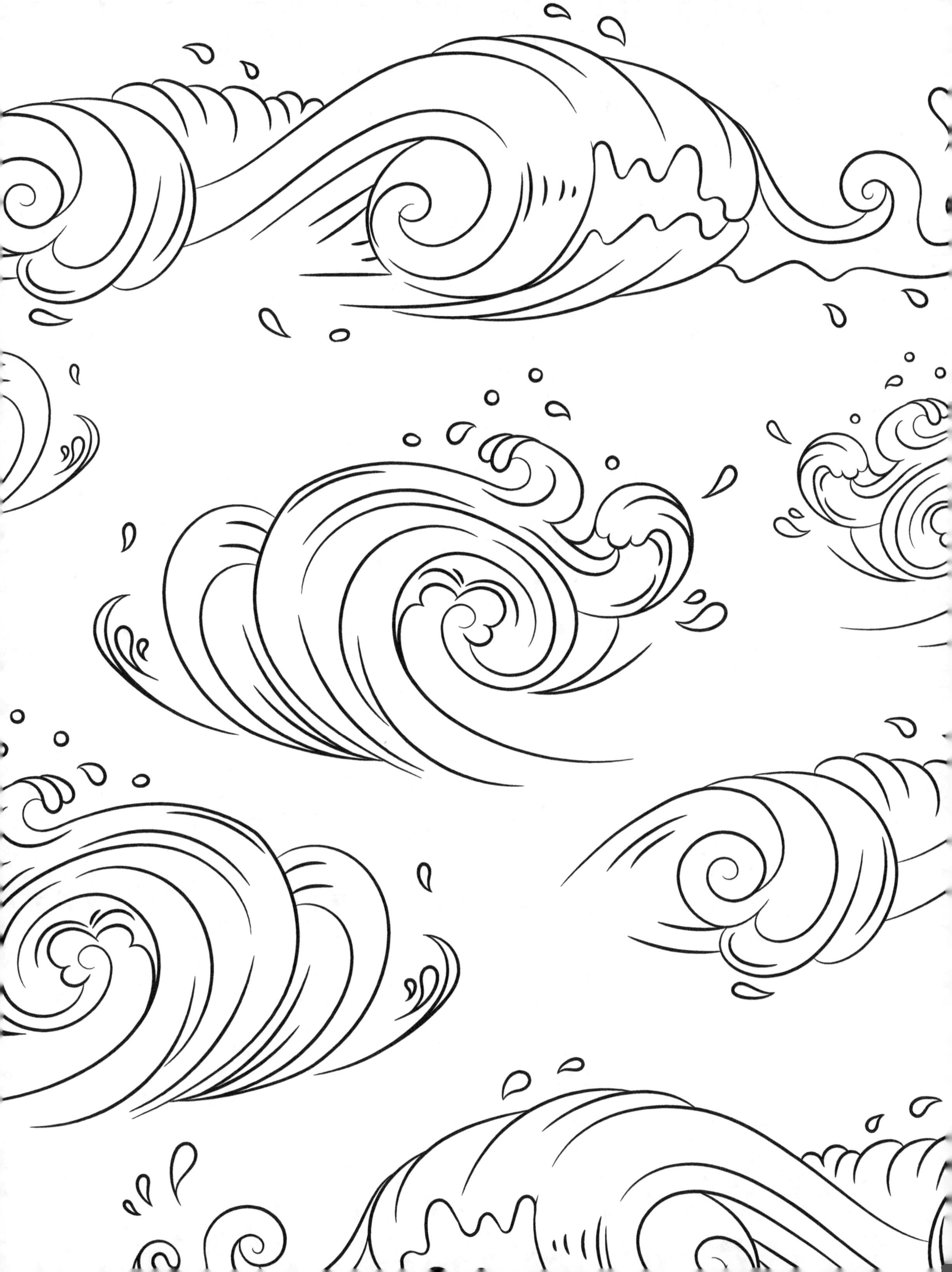

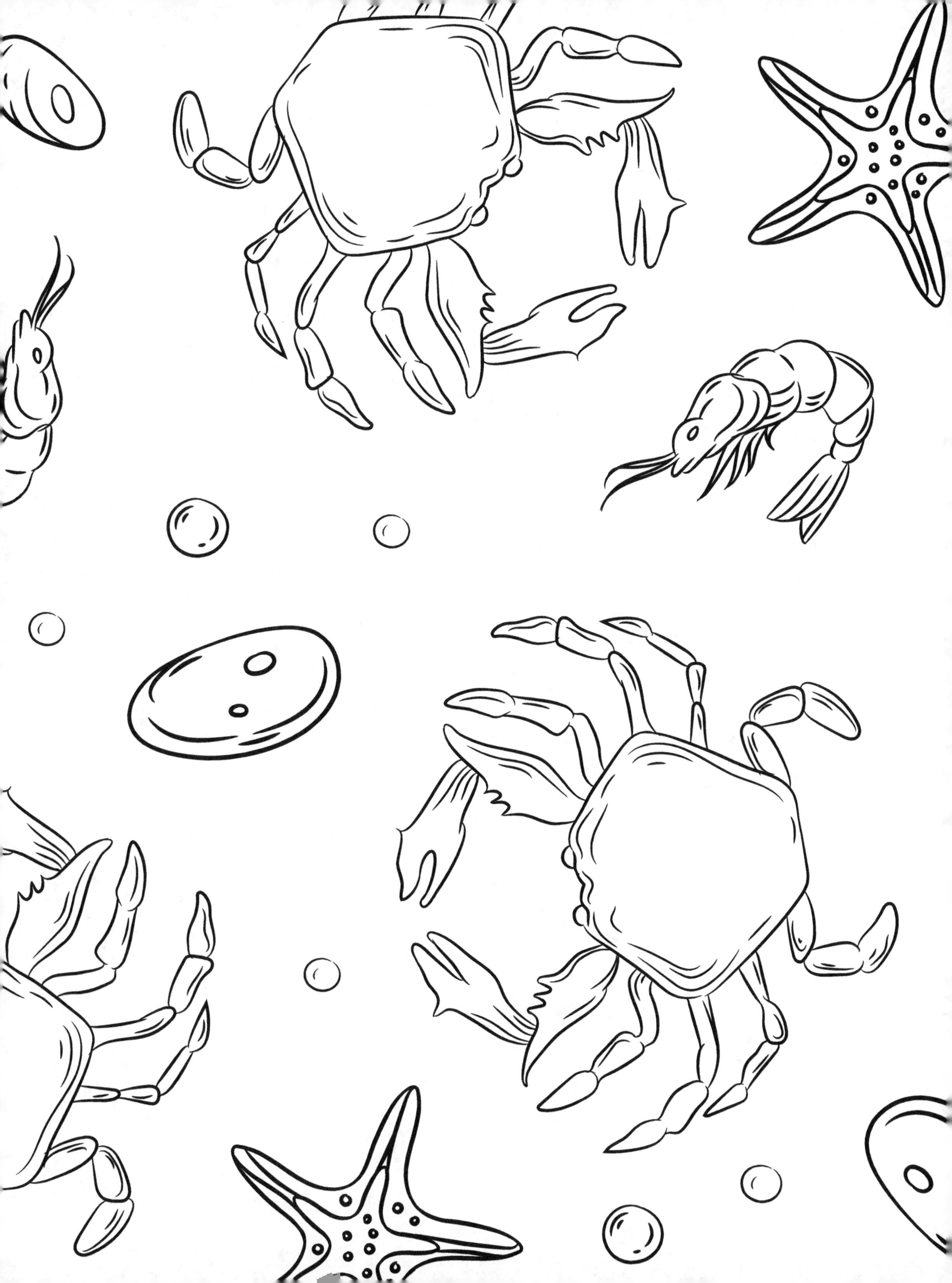

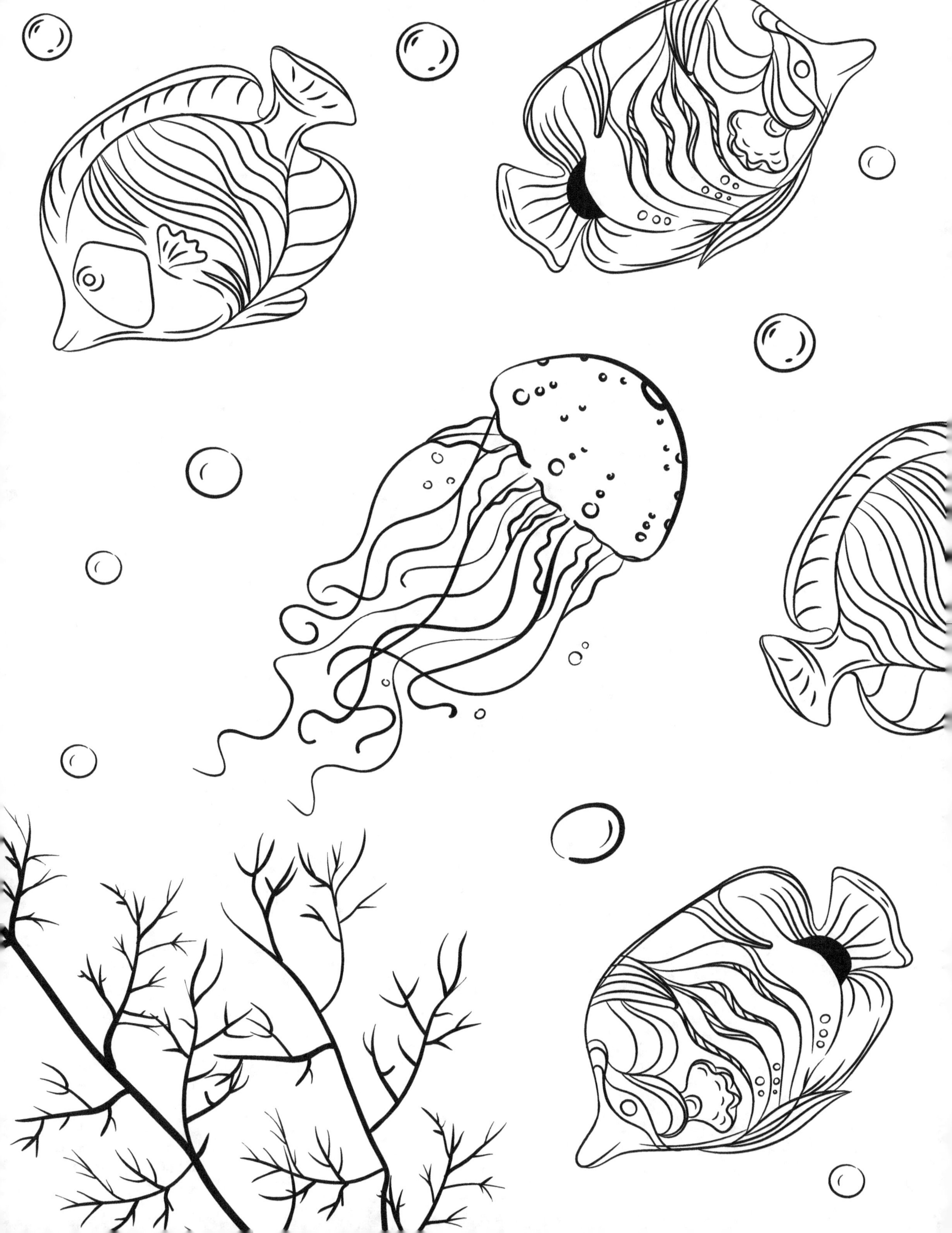

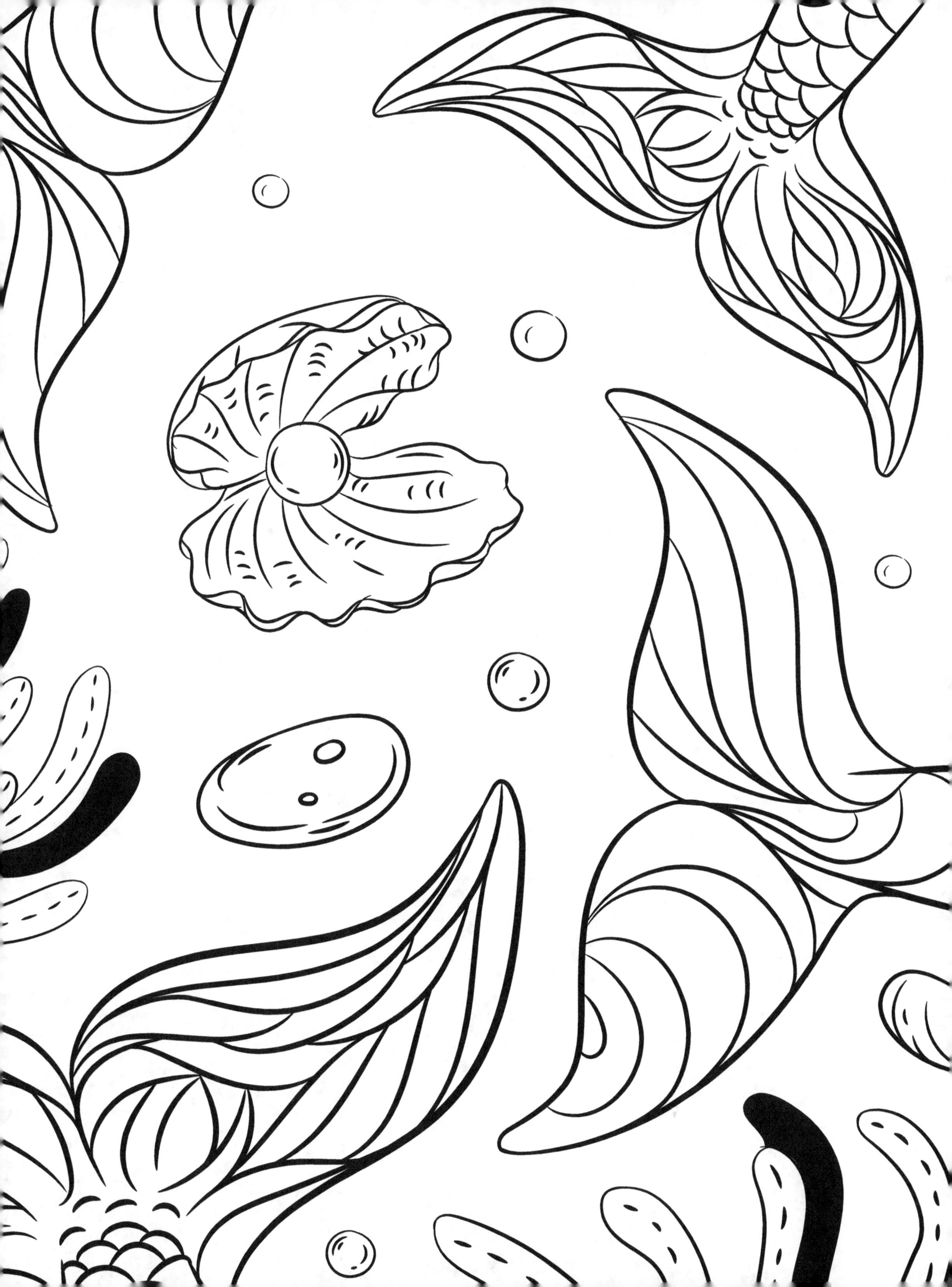

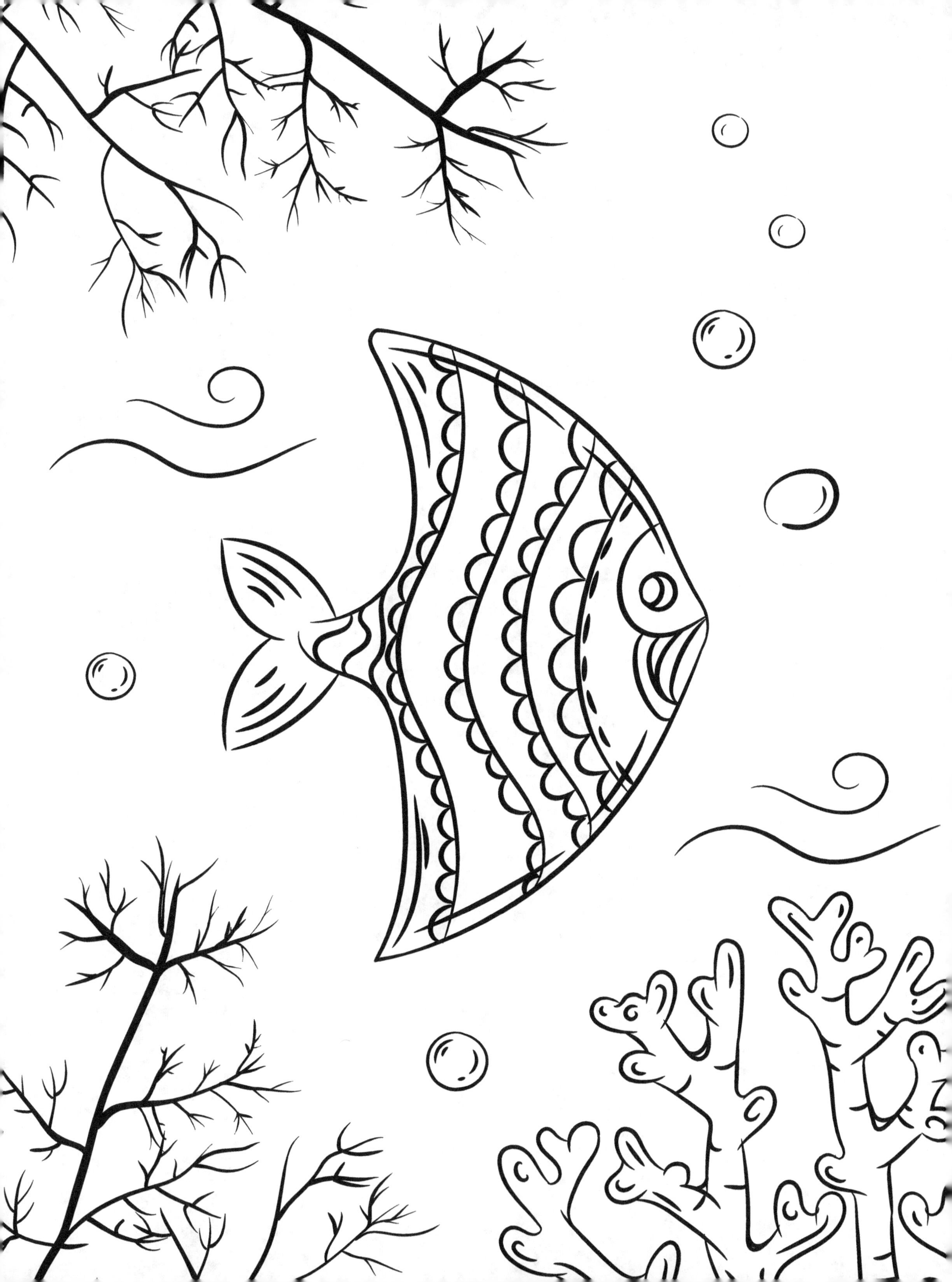

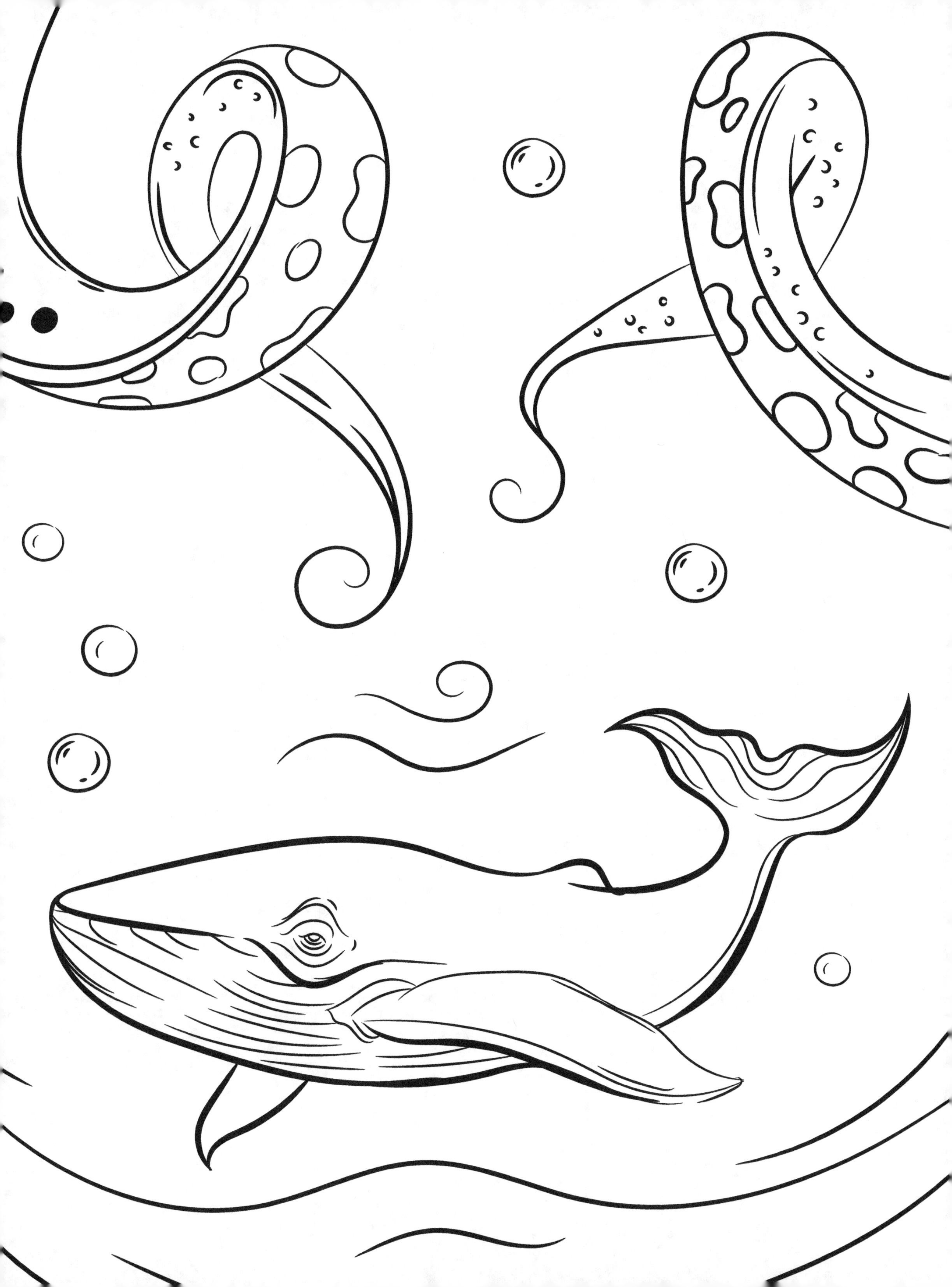

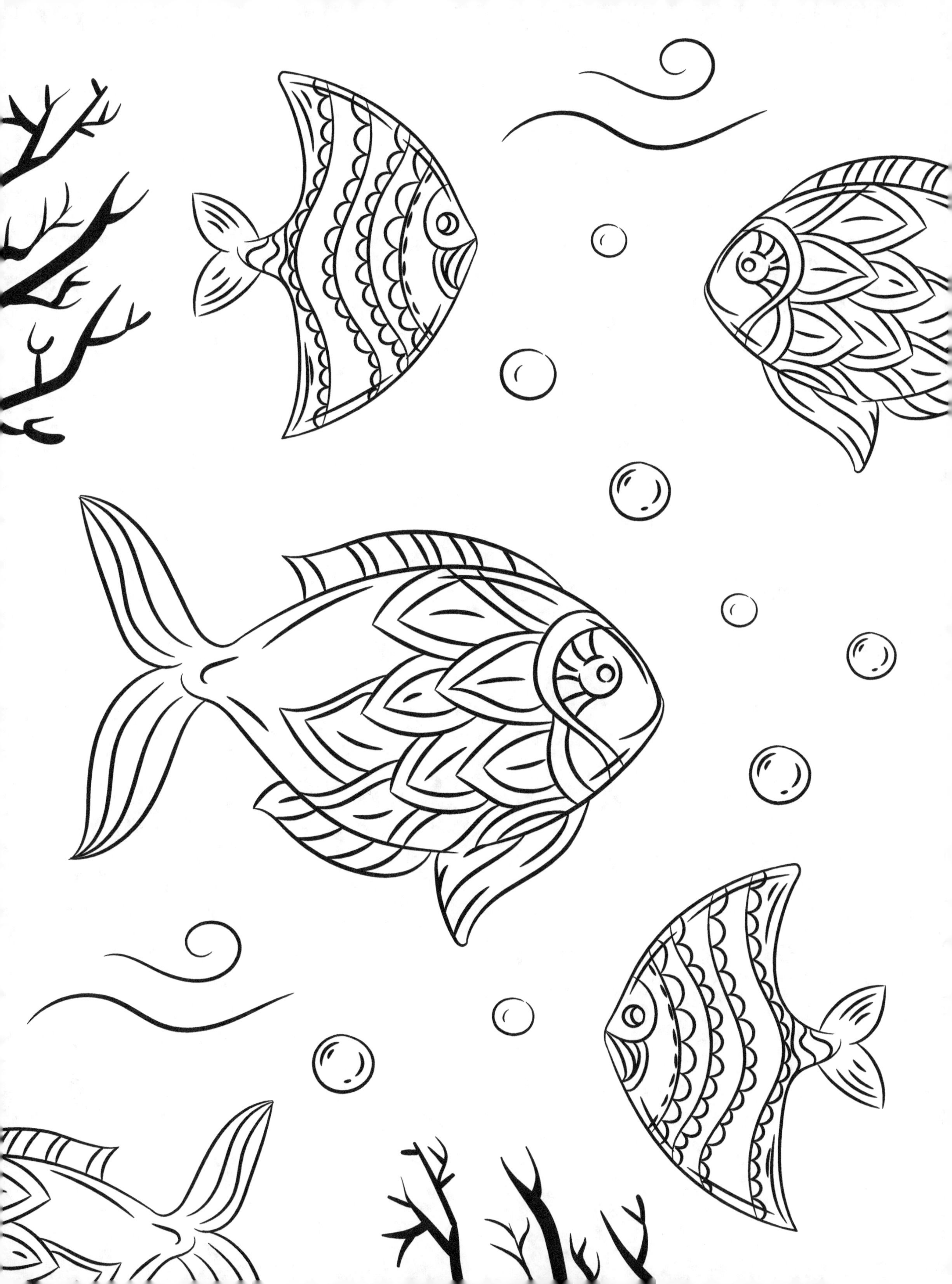

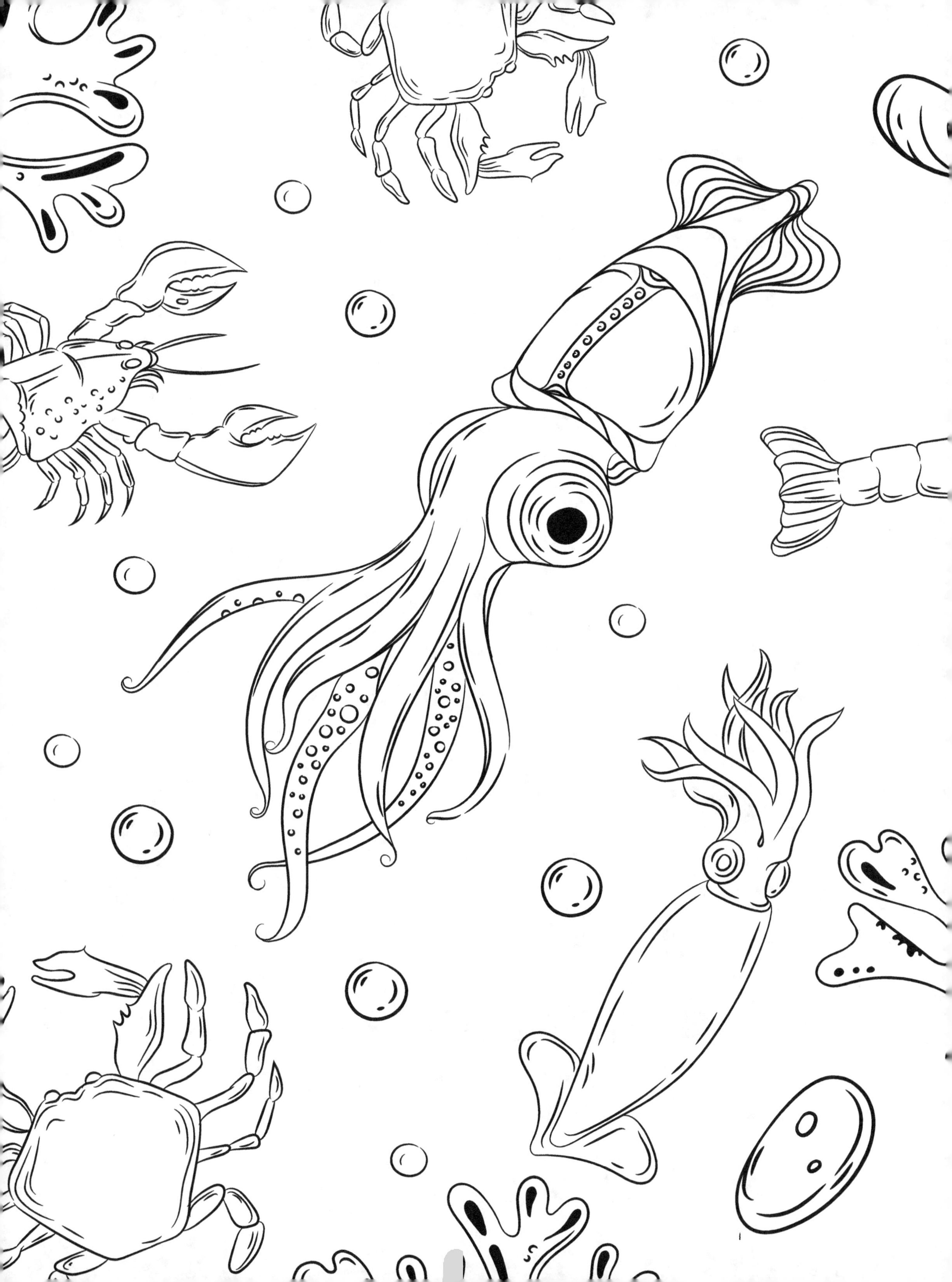

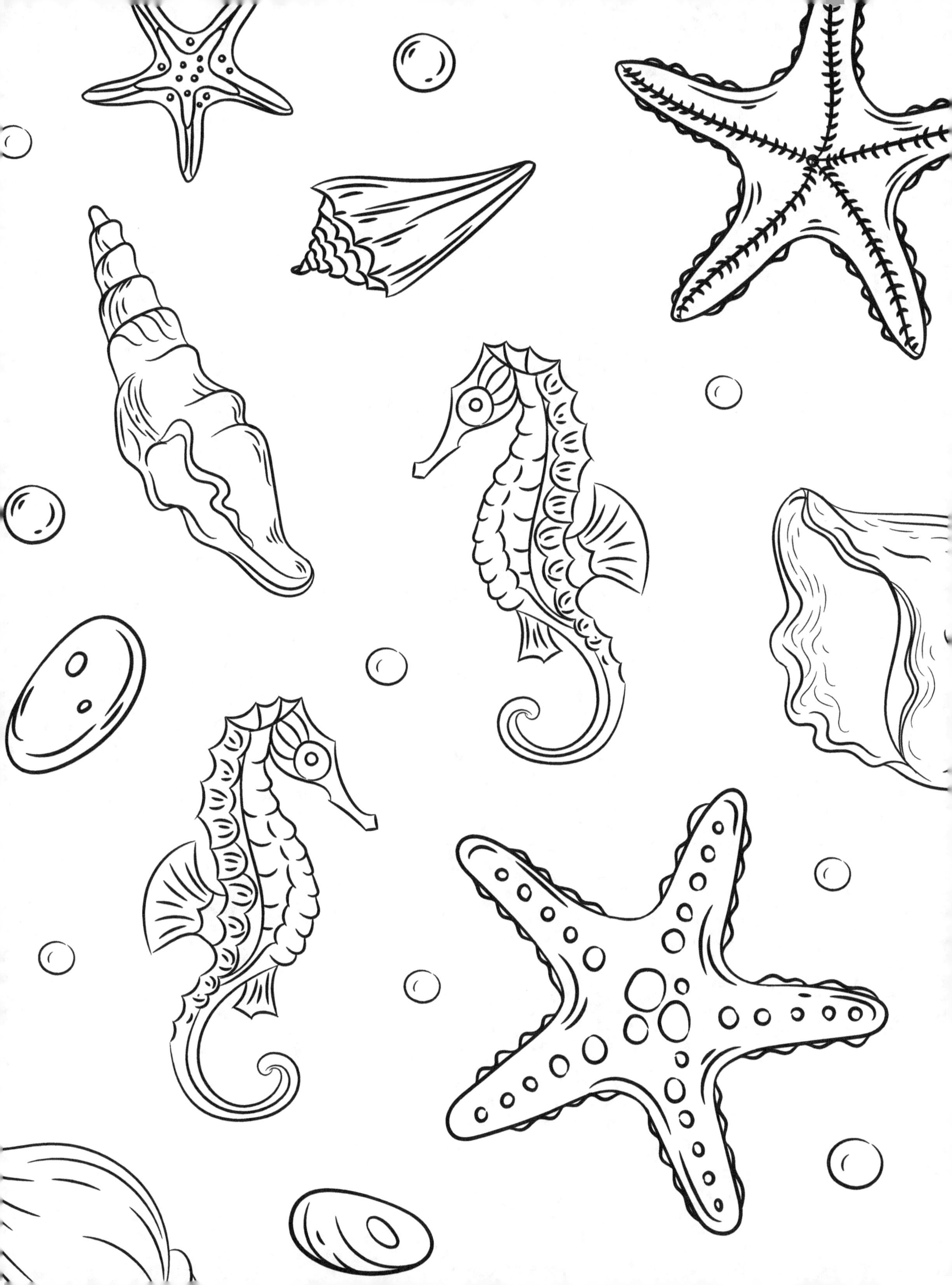

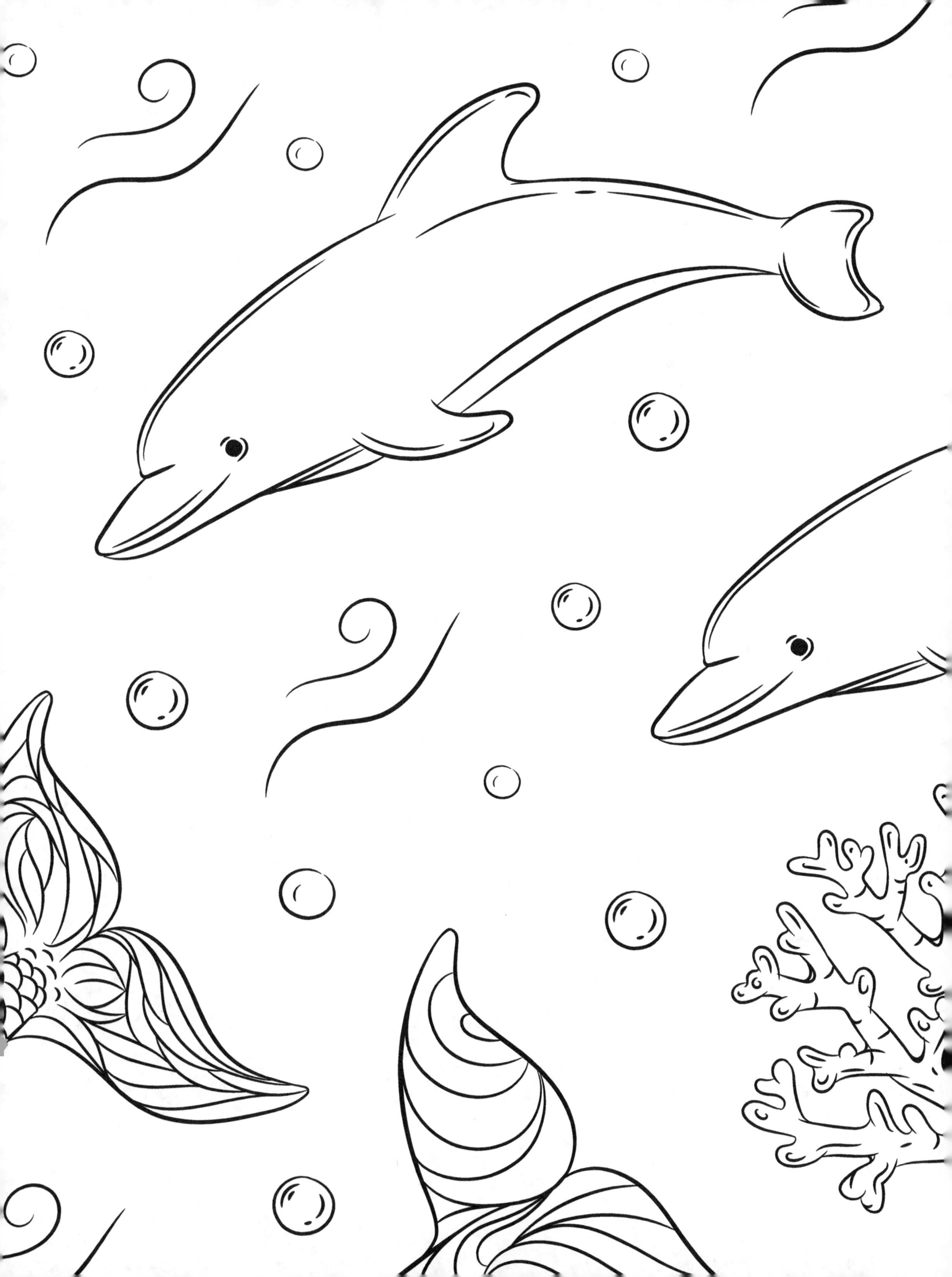

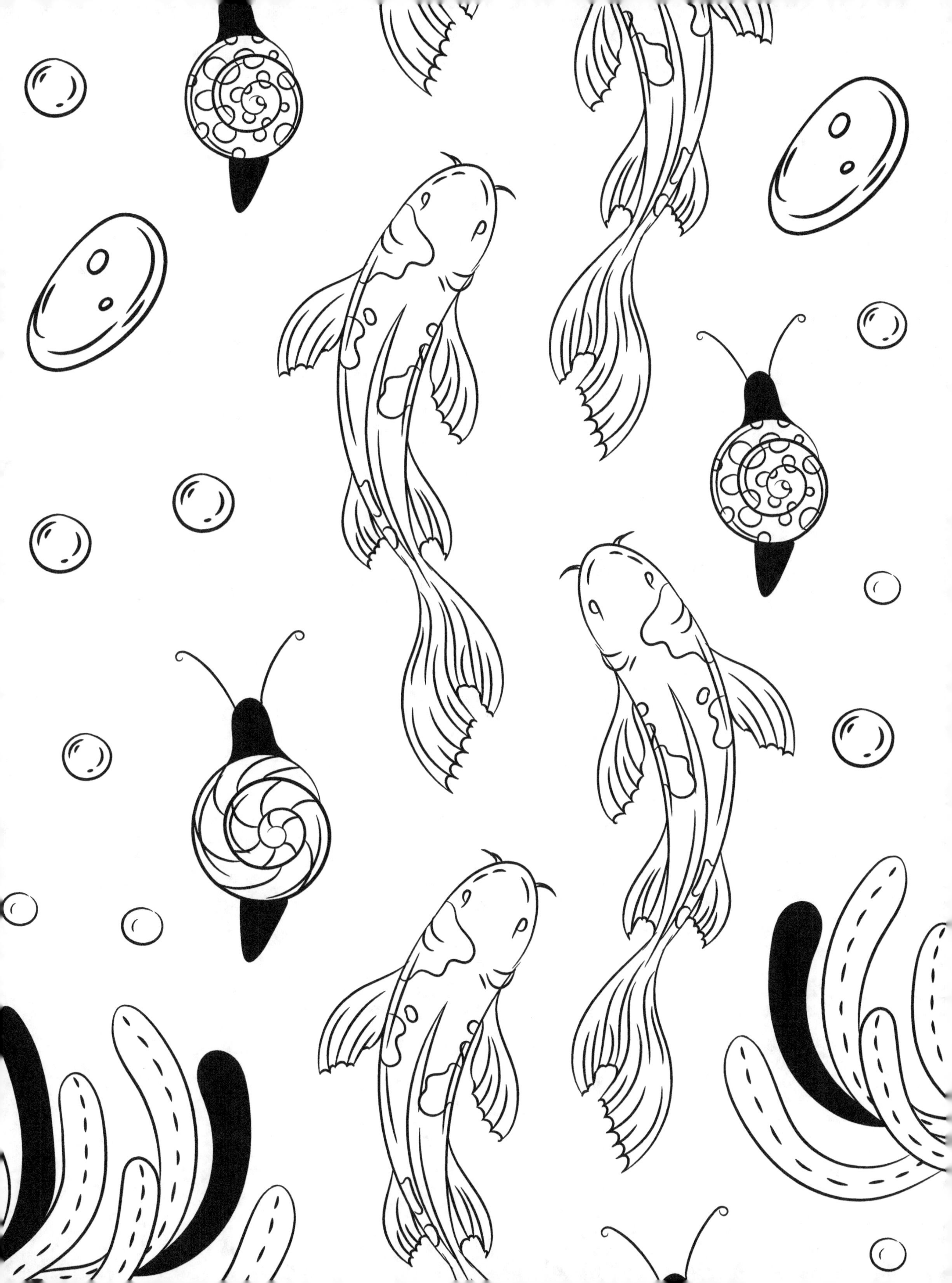

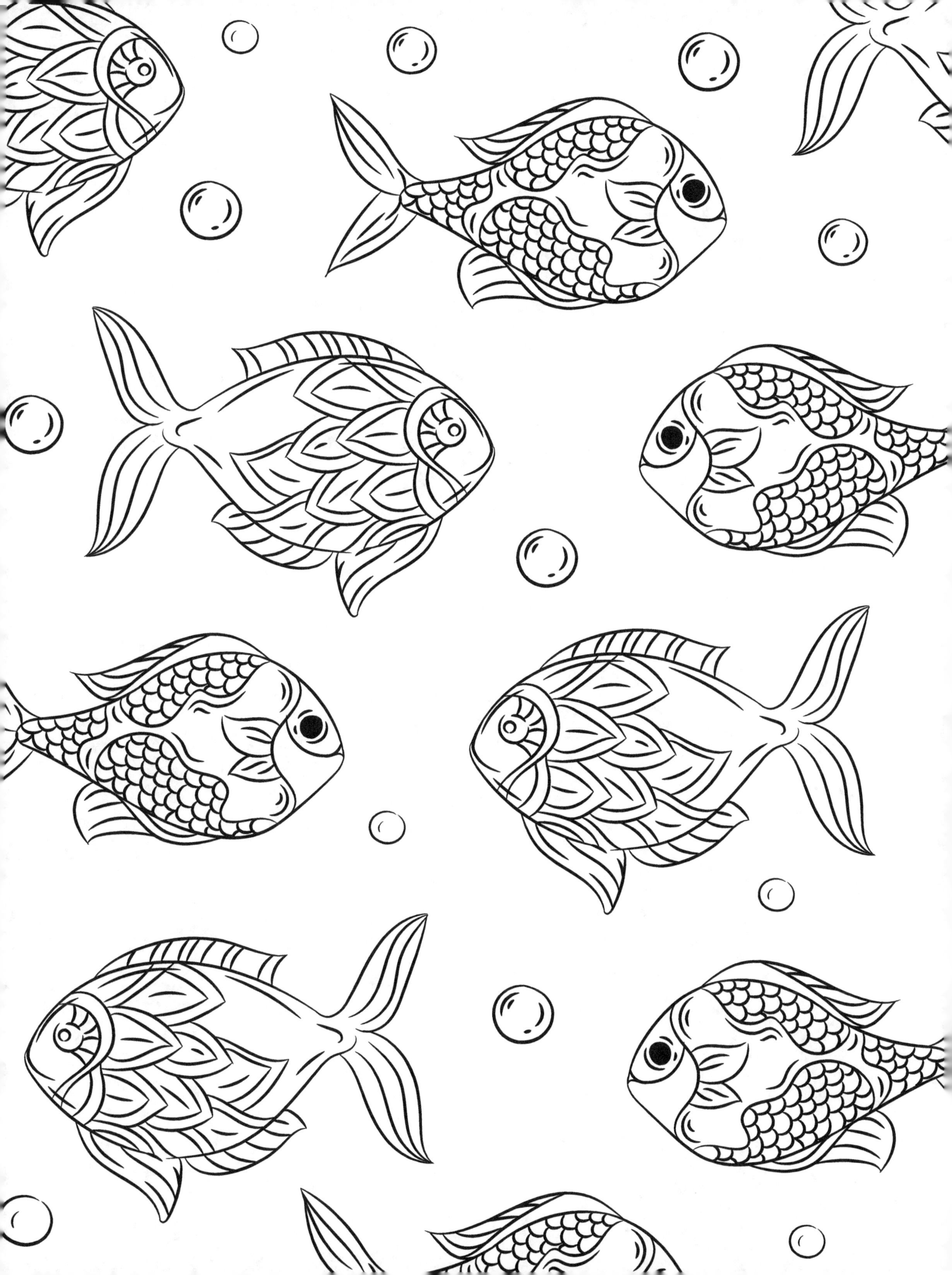

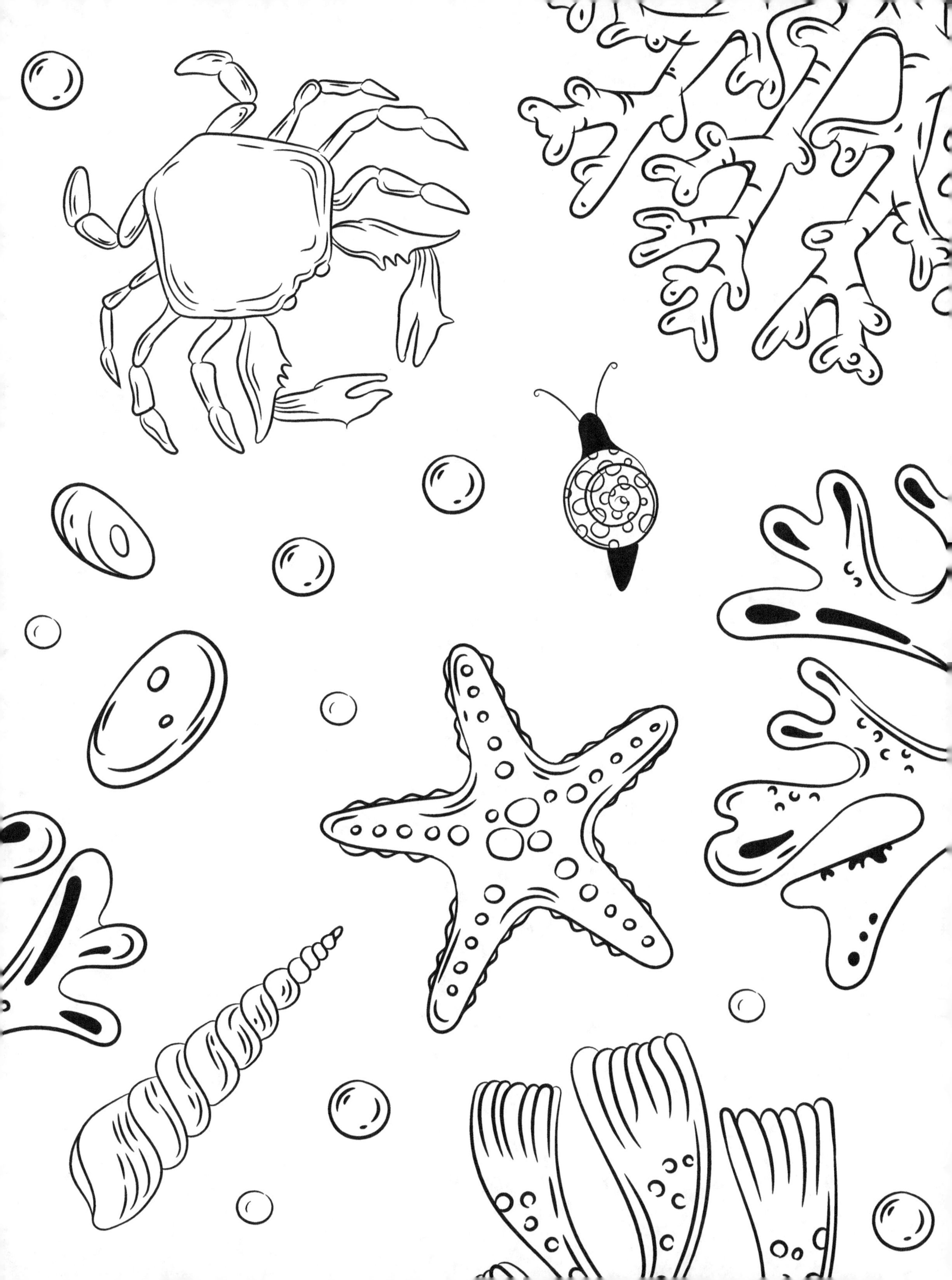

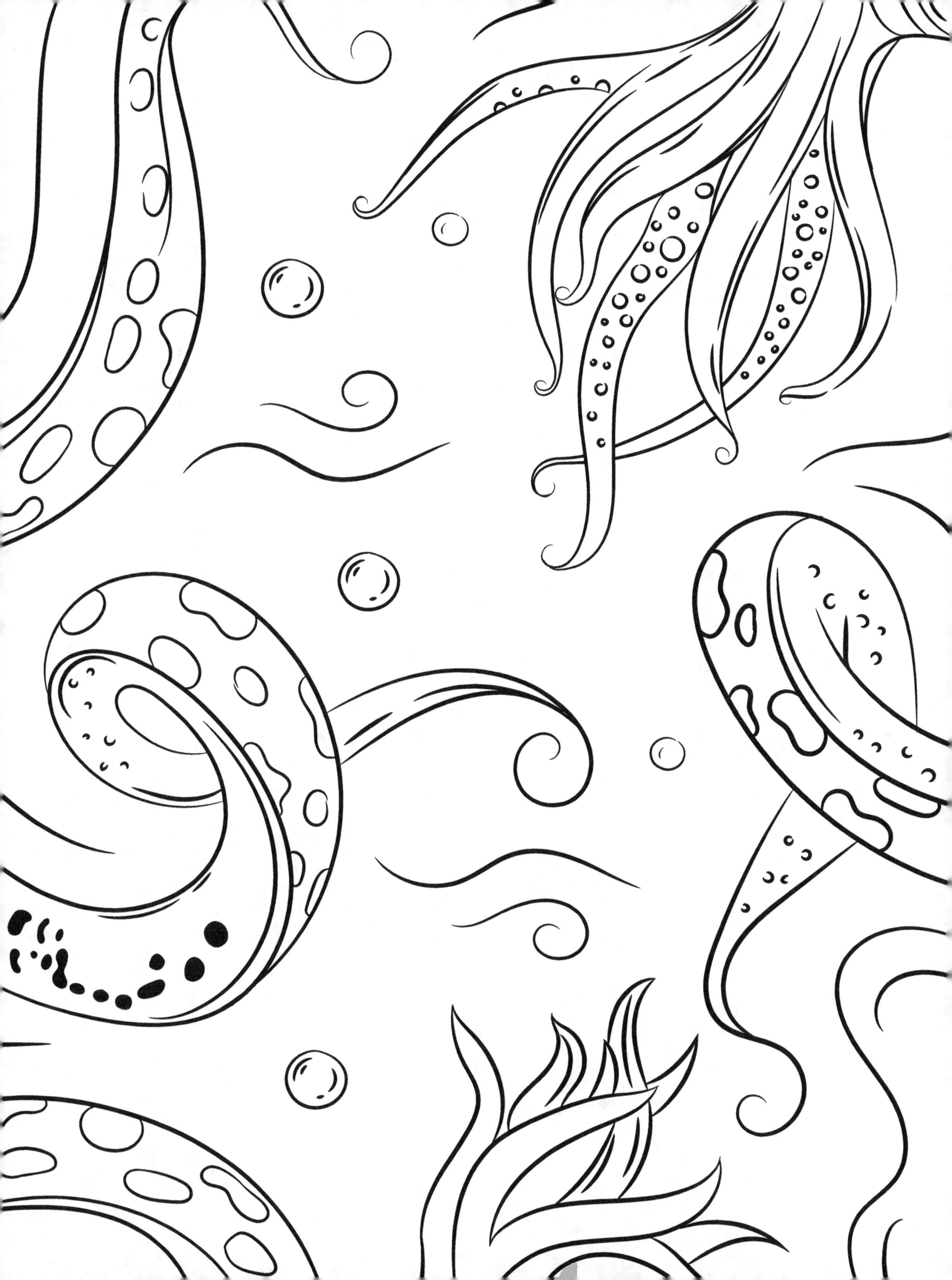

www.ingramcontent.com/pod-product-compliance
Lightning Source LLC
Chambersburg PA
CBHW081656220526
45466CB00009B/2776
9781677812004